ANYONE CAN DRAW CUTE ANIMALS

For Kids

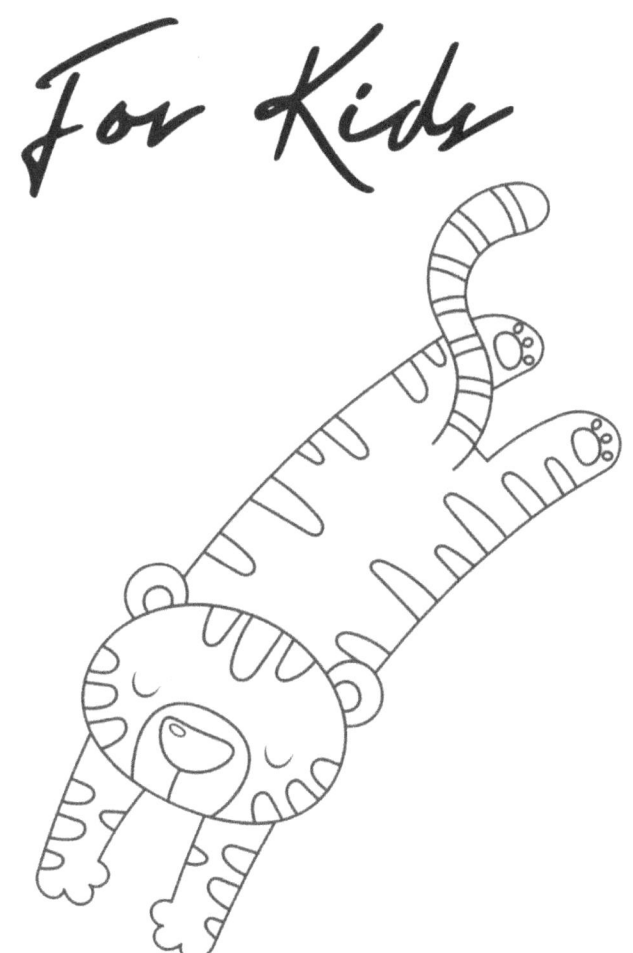

All rights reserved, No part of this publication may be reproduced distributed or transmitted in any form or by any means including photocopying recording, or other electronic or mechanical methods

How to draw a giraffe

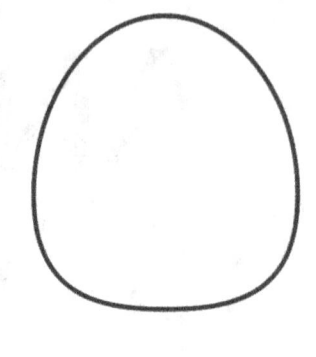
1.

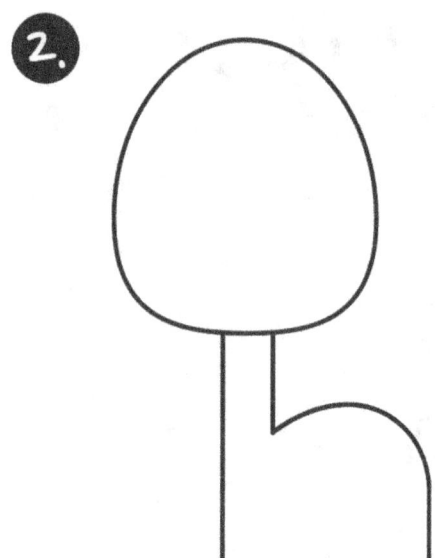
2.

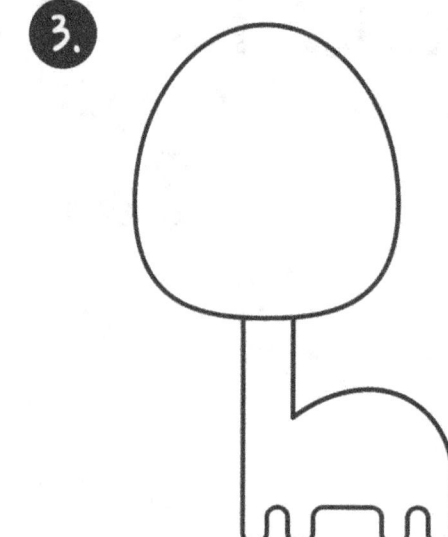
3.

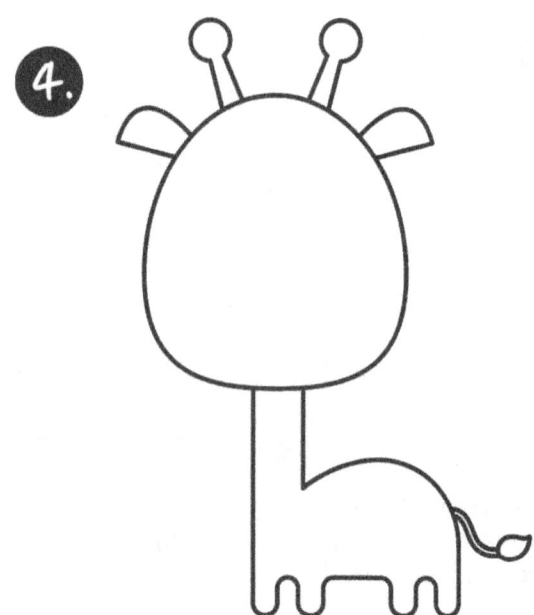
4.

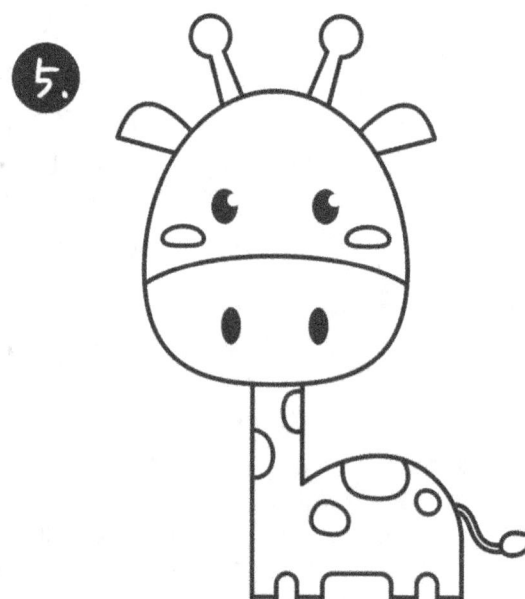
5.

YOUR TURN

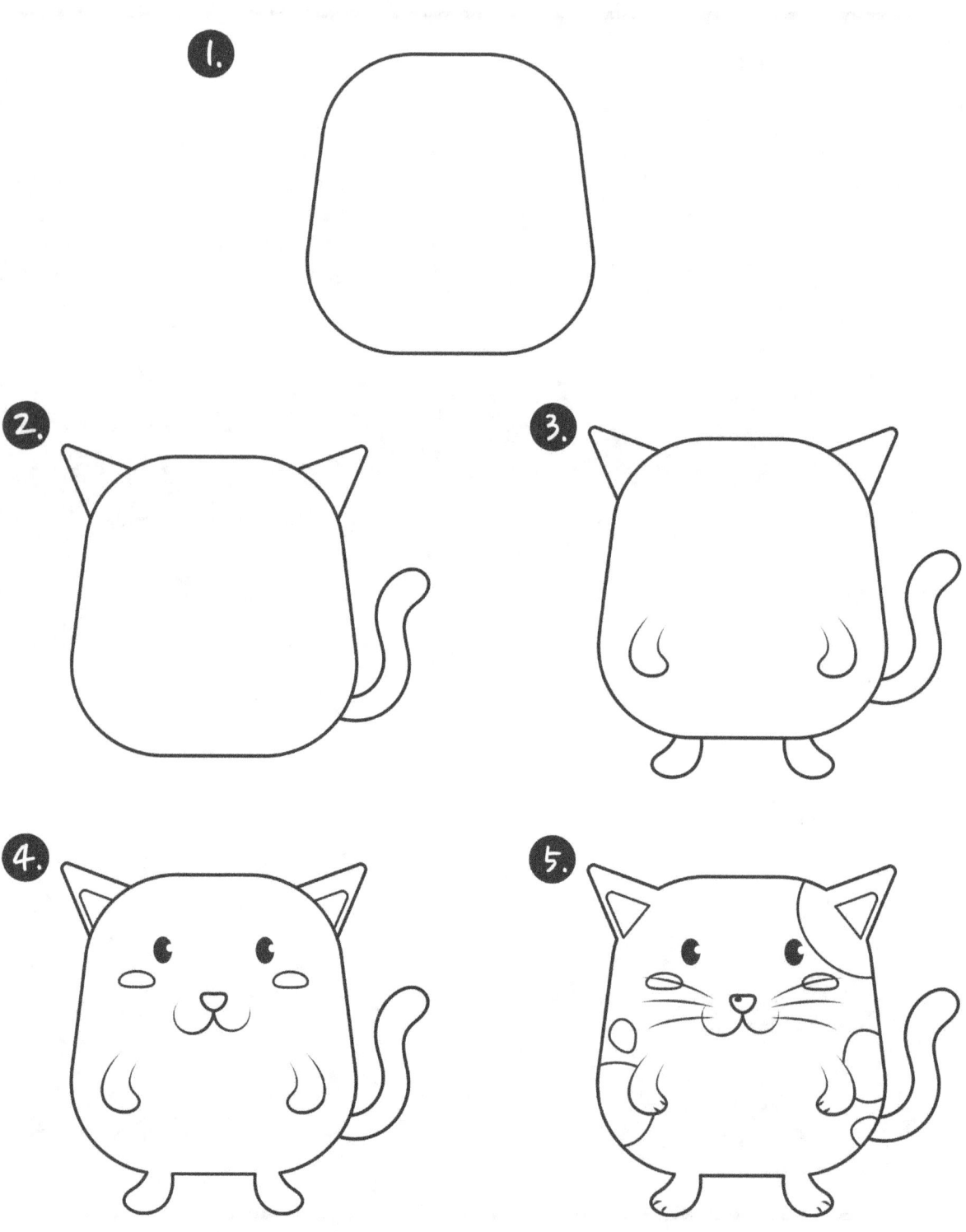

YOUR TURN

How to draw easy tiger

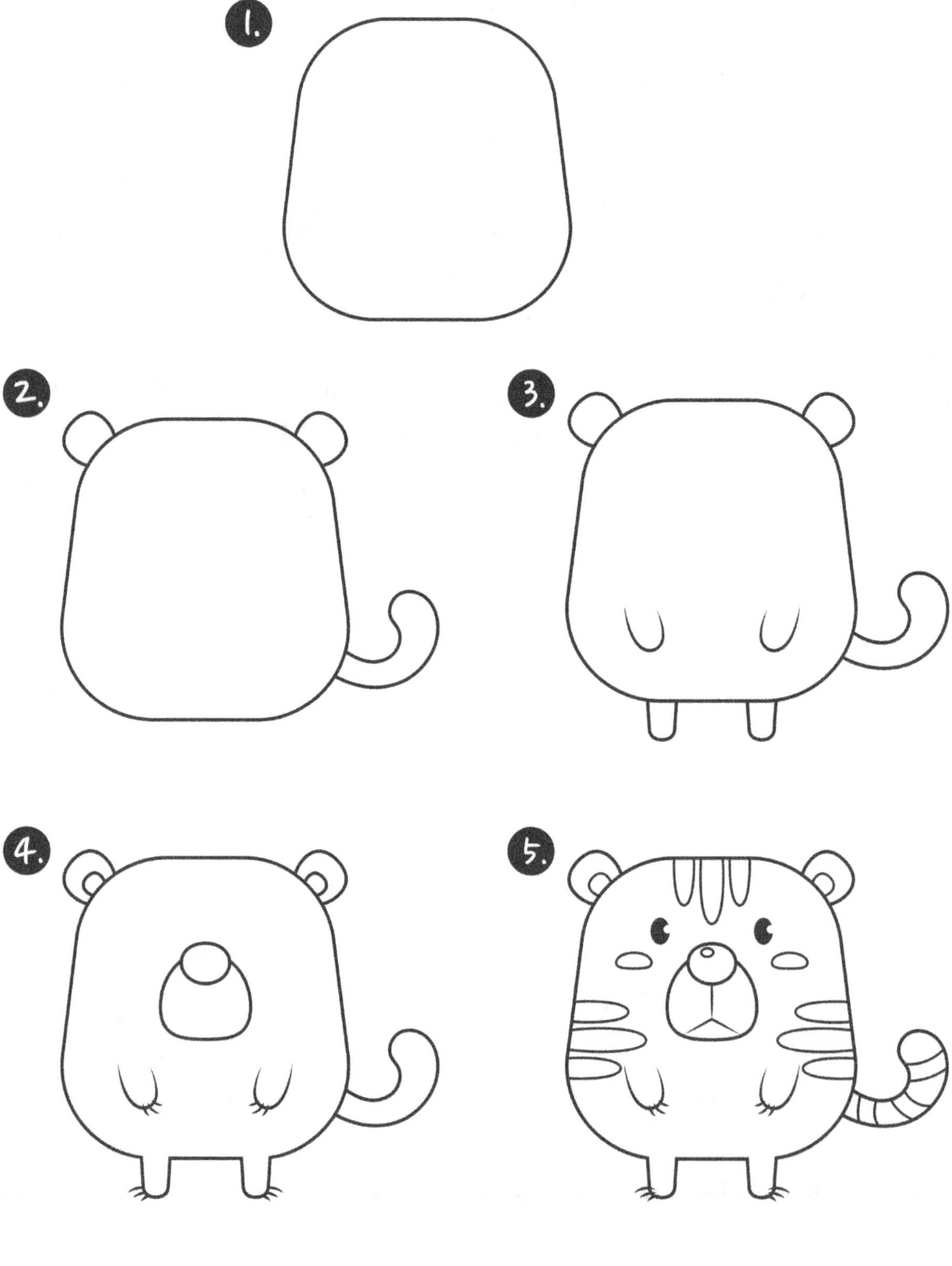

1.
2.
3.
4.
5.

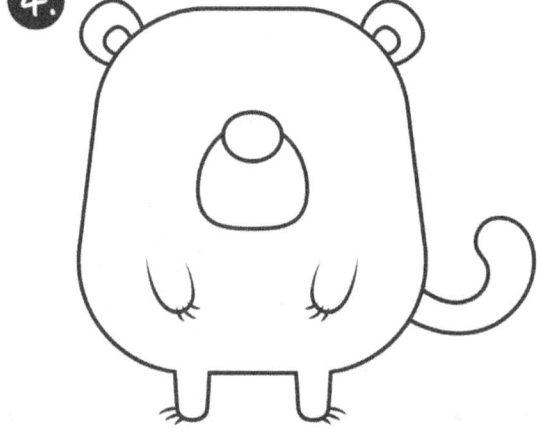
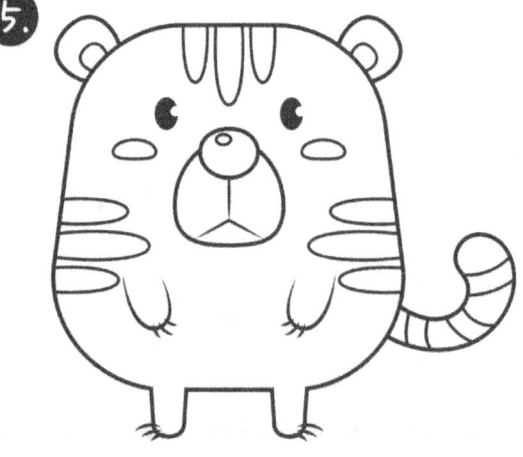

YOUR TURN

How to draw fat dog

1.
2.
3.
4.
5.

YOUR TURN

How to draw fat dinosaur

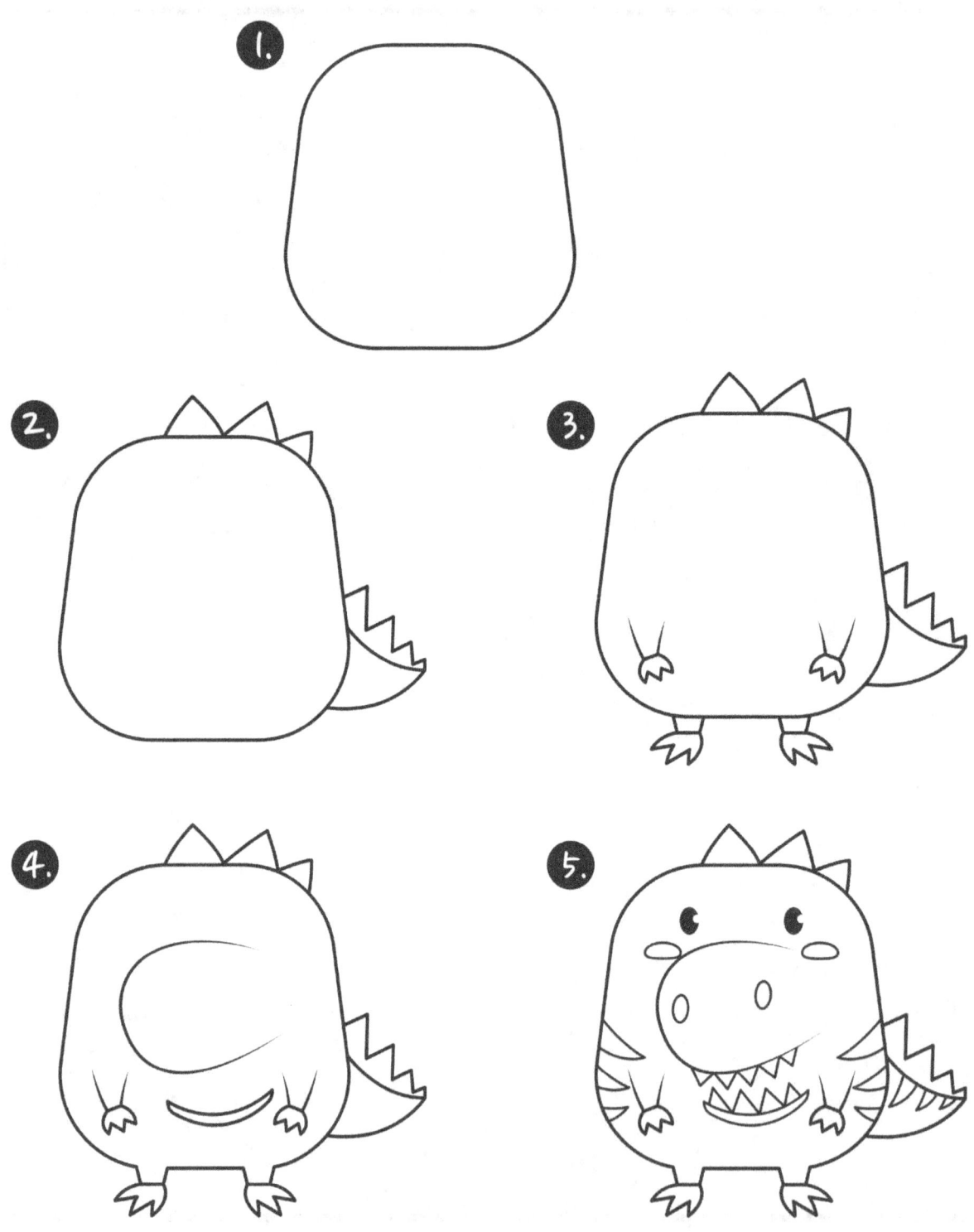

YOUR TURN

How to draw easy squirrel

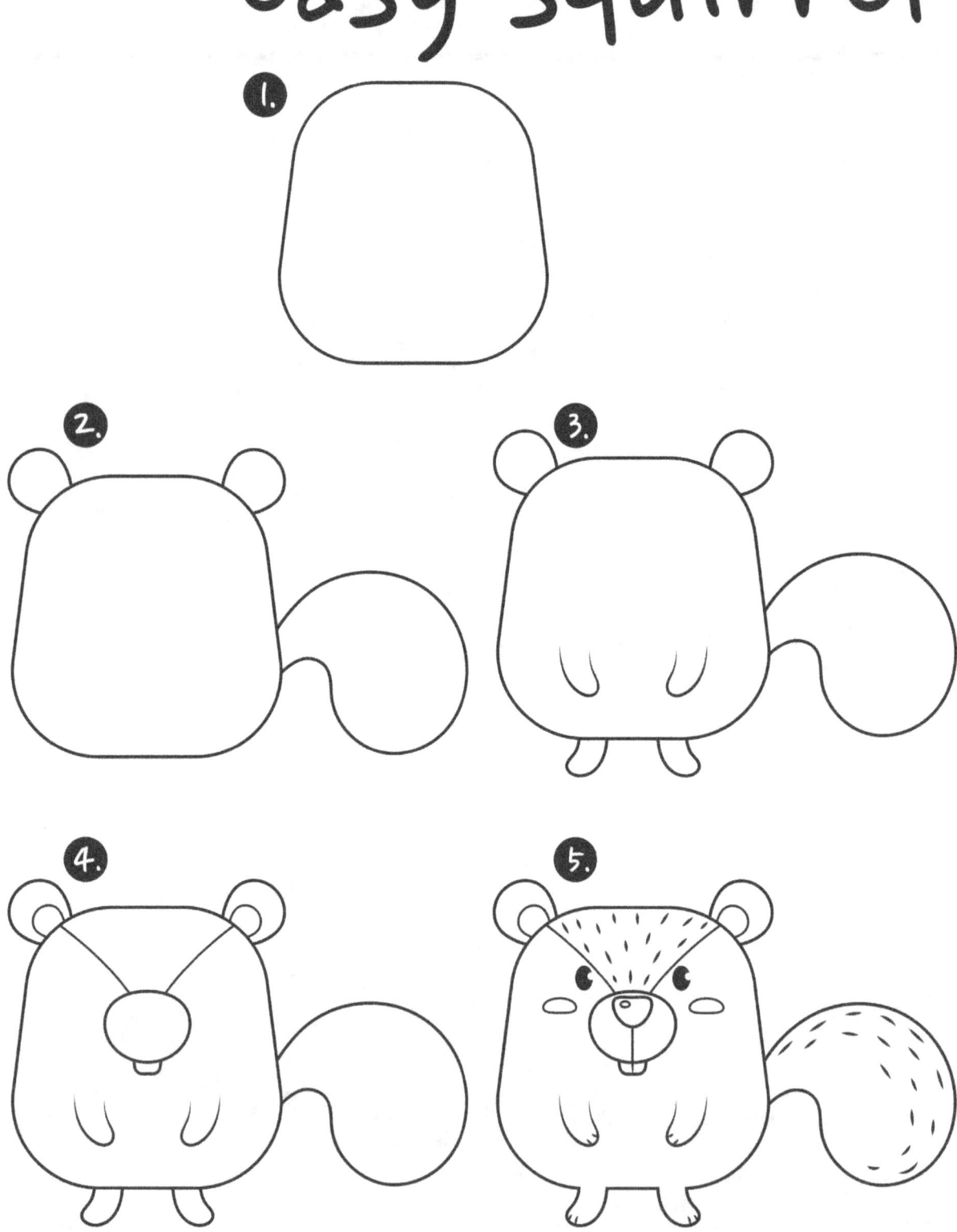

YOUR TURN

How to draw easy Pig

1.
2.
3.
4.
5.

YOUR TURN

How to draw easy bunny

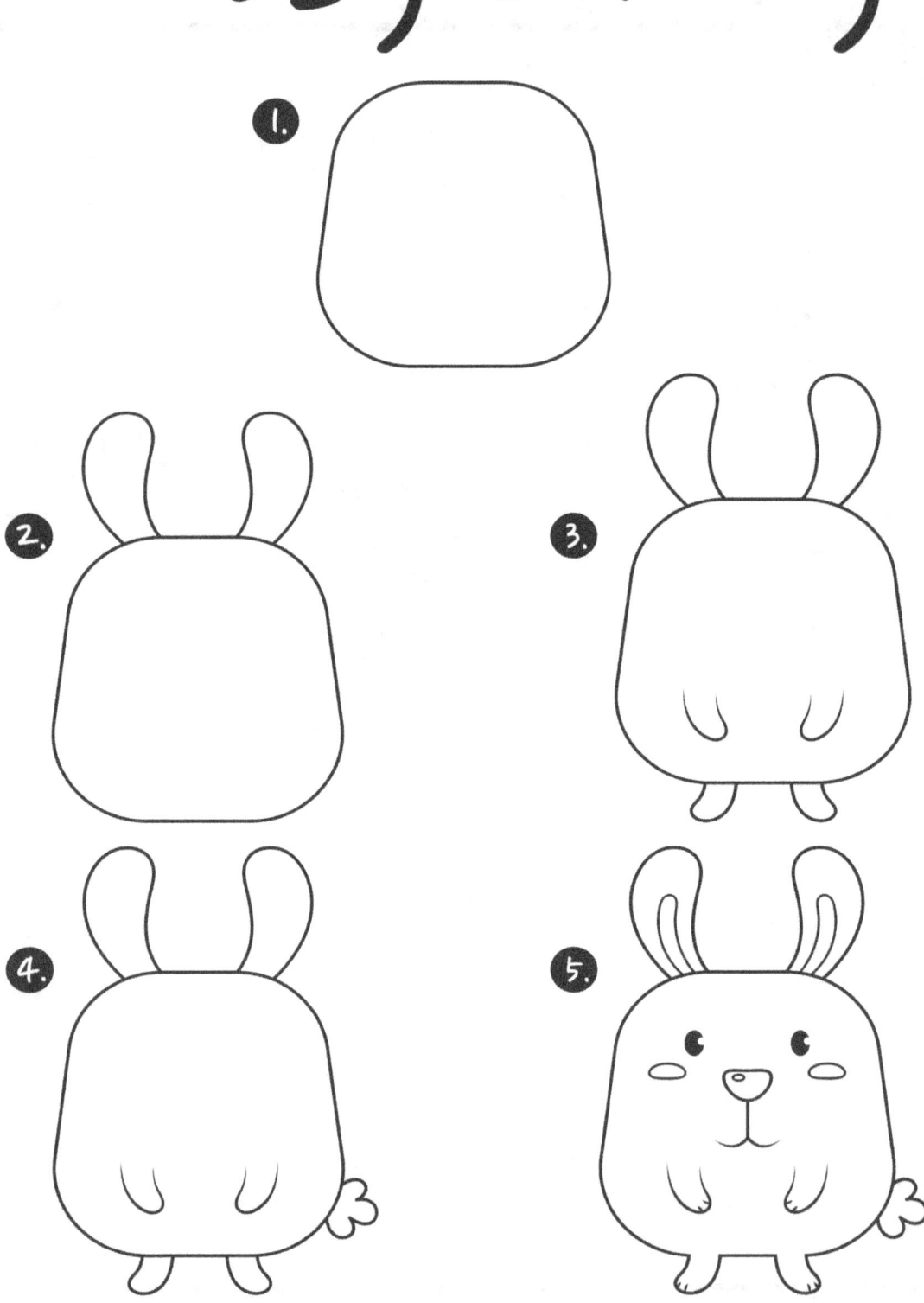

YOUR TURN

How to draw an owl

1.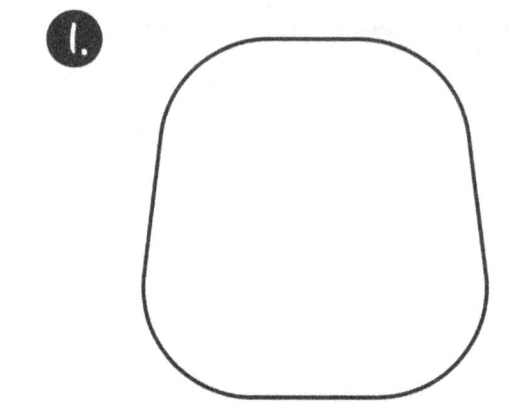
2.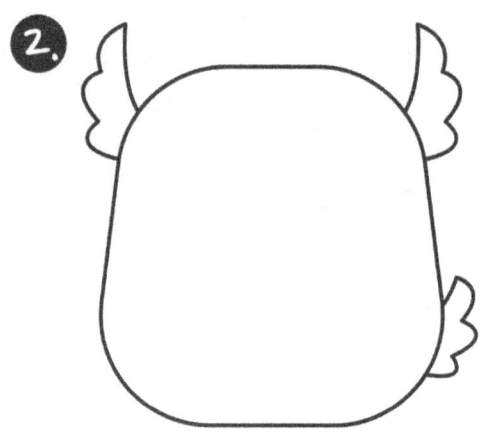
3.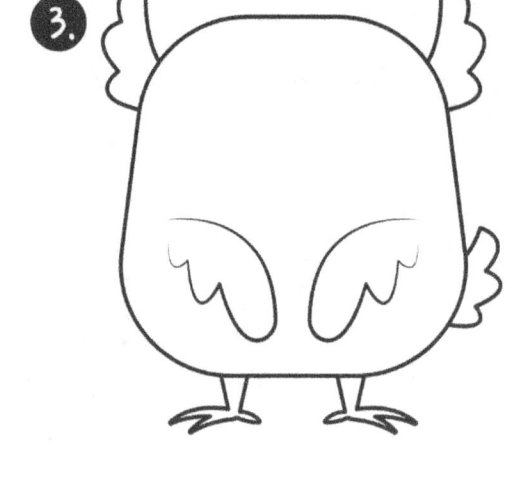
4.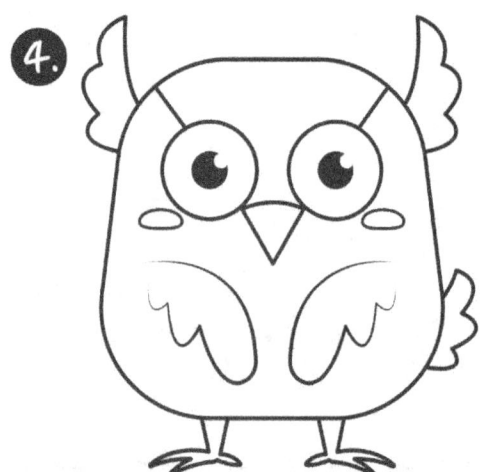
5.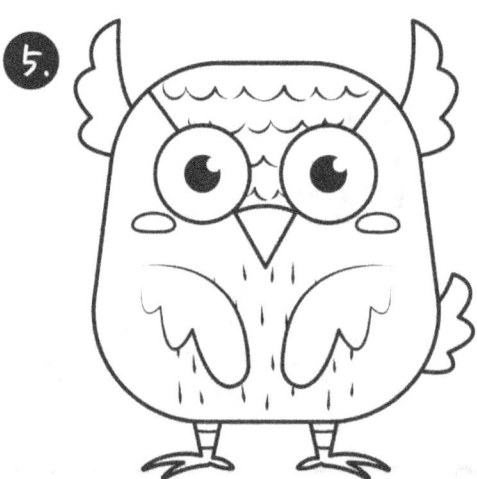

YOUR TURN

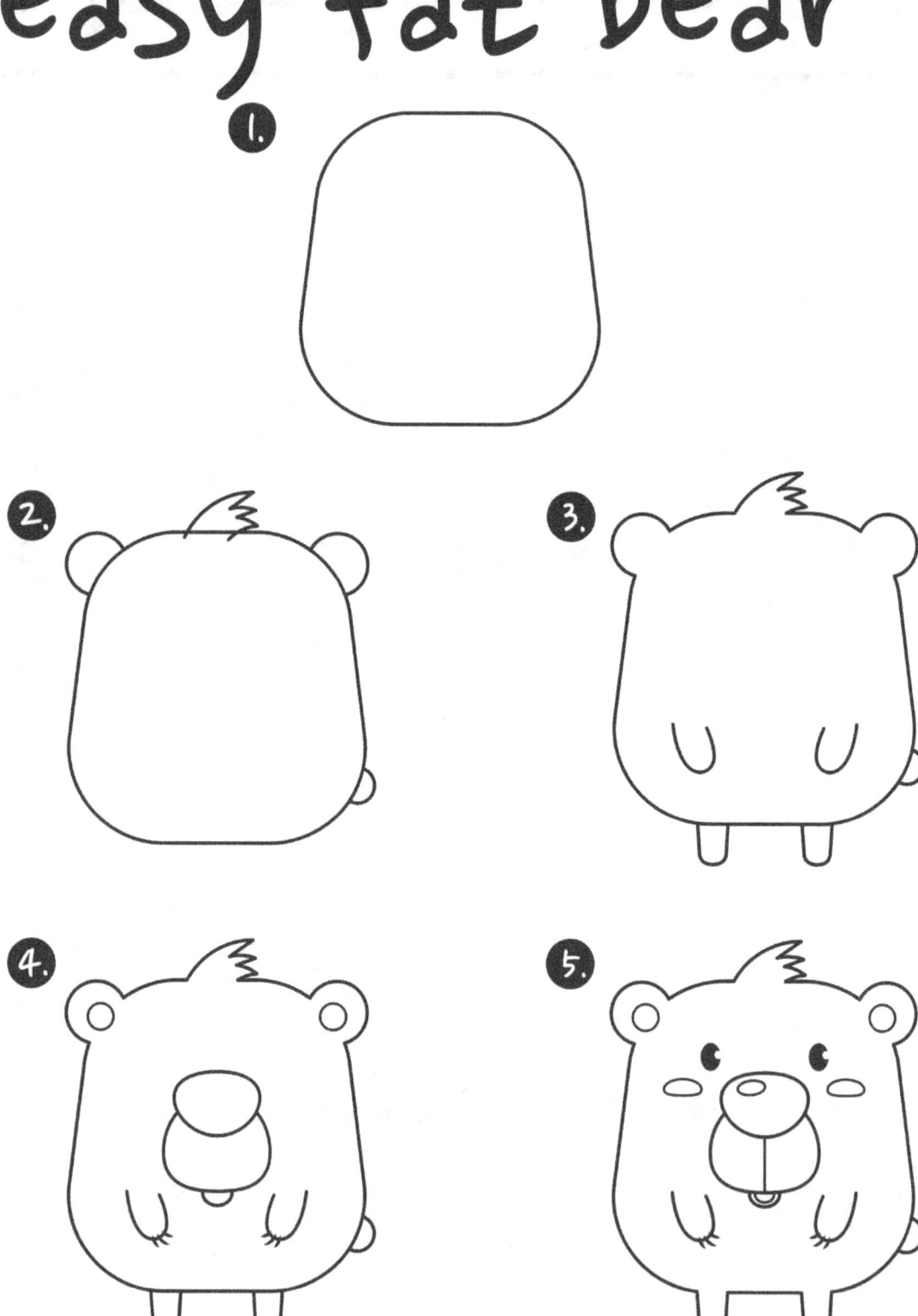

YOUR TURN

How to draw a mouse

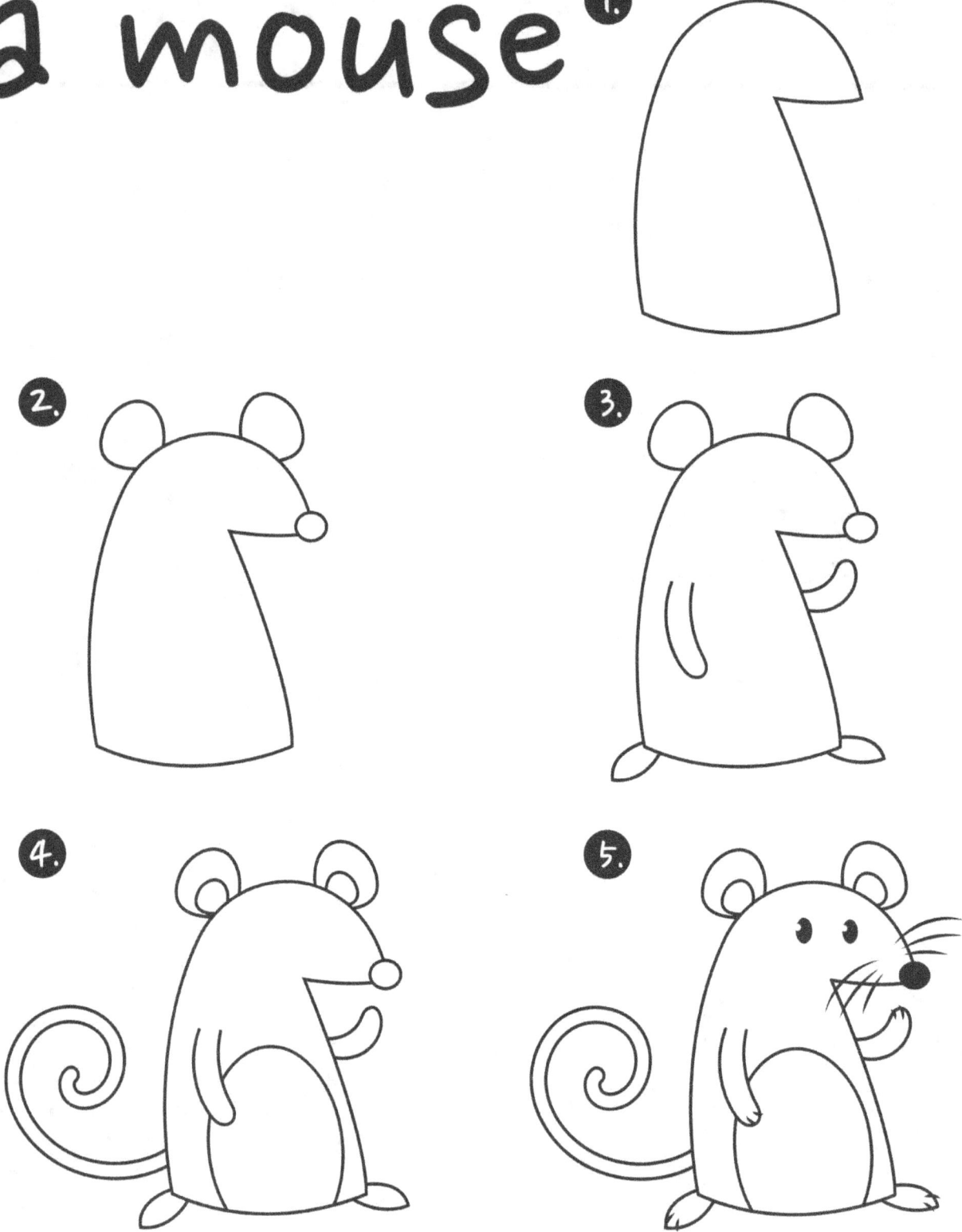

YOUR TURN

How to draw sleeping cat

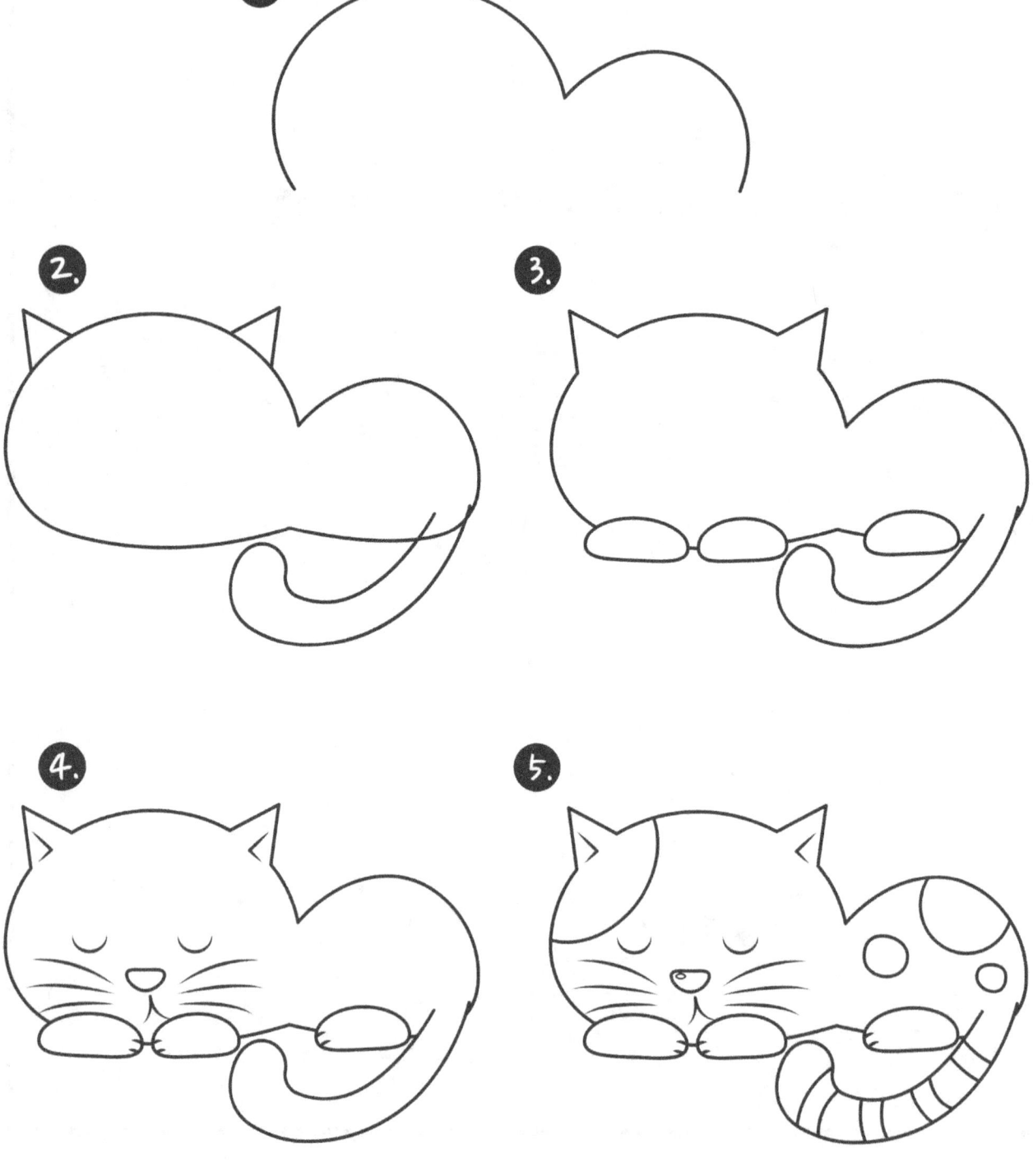

How to draw a bull

1.
2.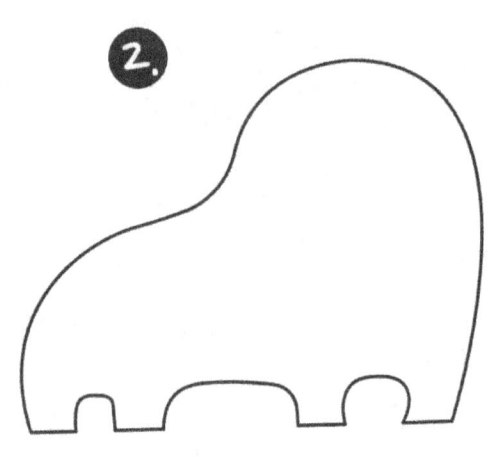
3.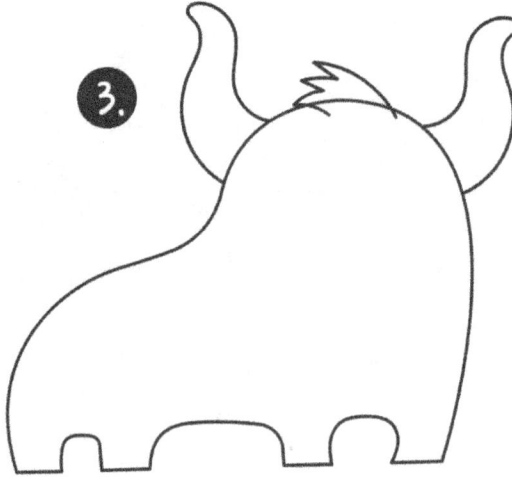
4.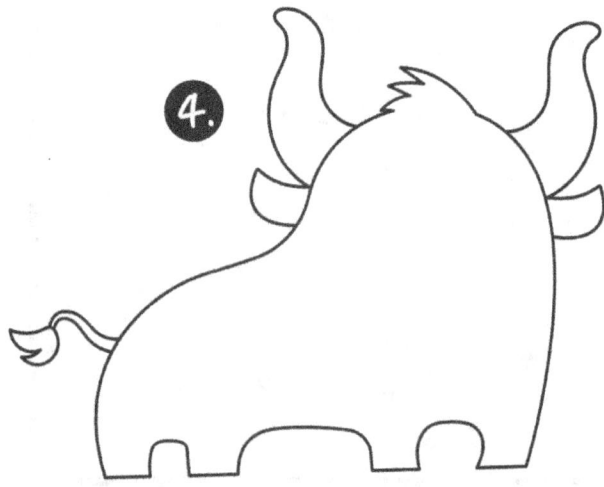
5.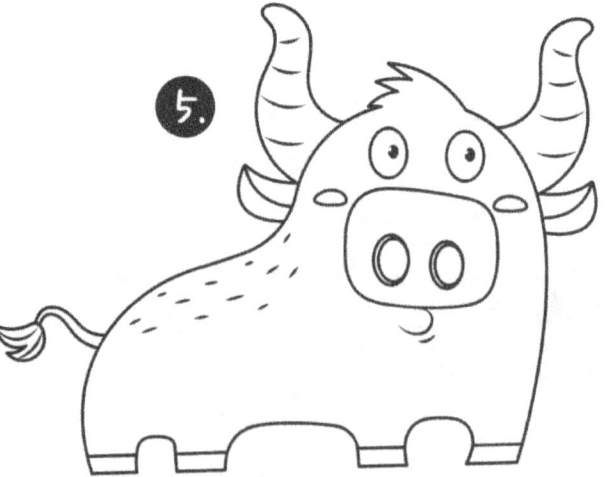

YOUR TURN

How to draw sea turtle

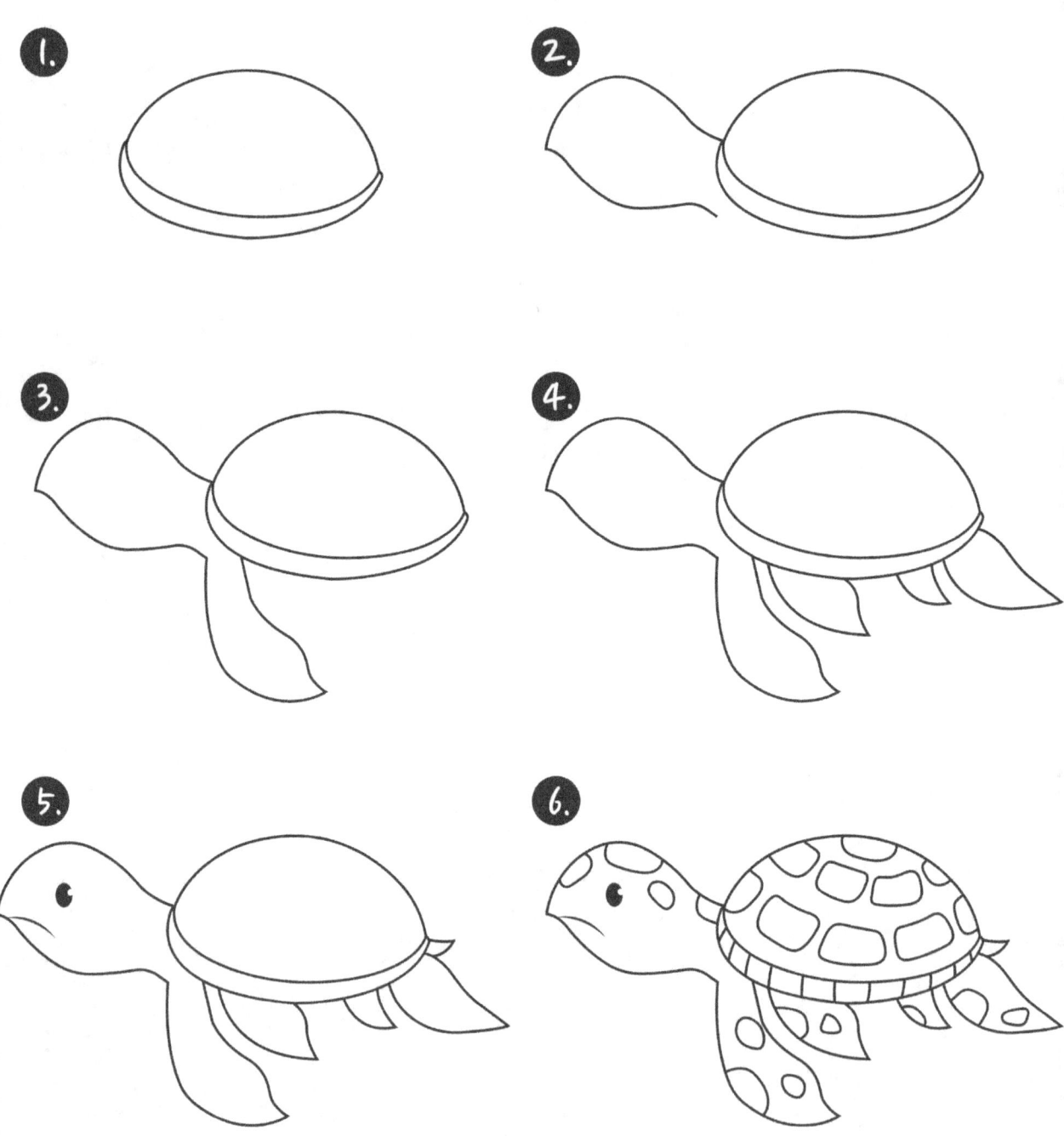

YOUR TURN

How to draw happy fox

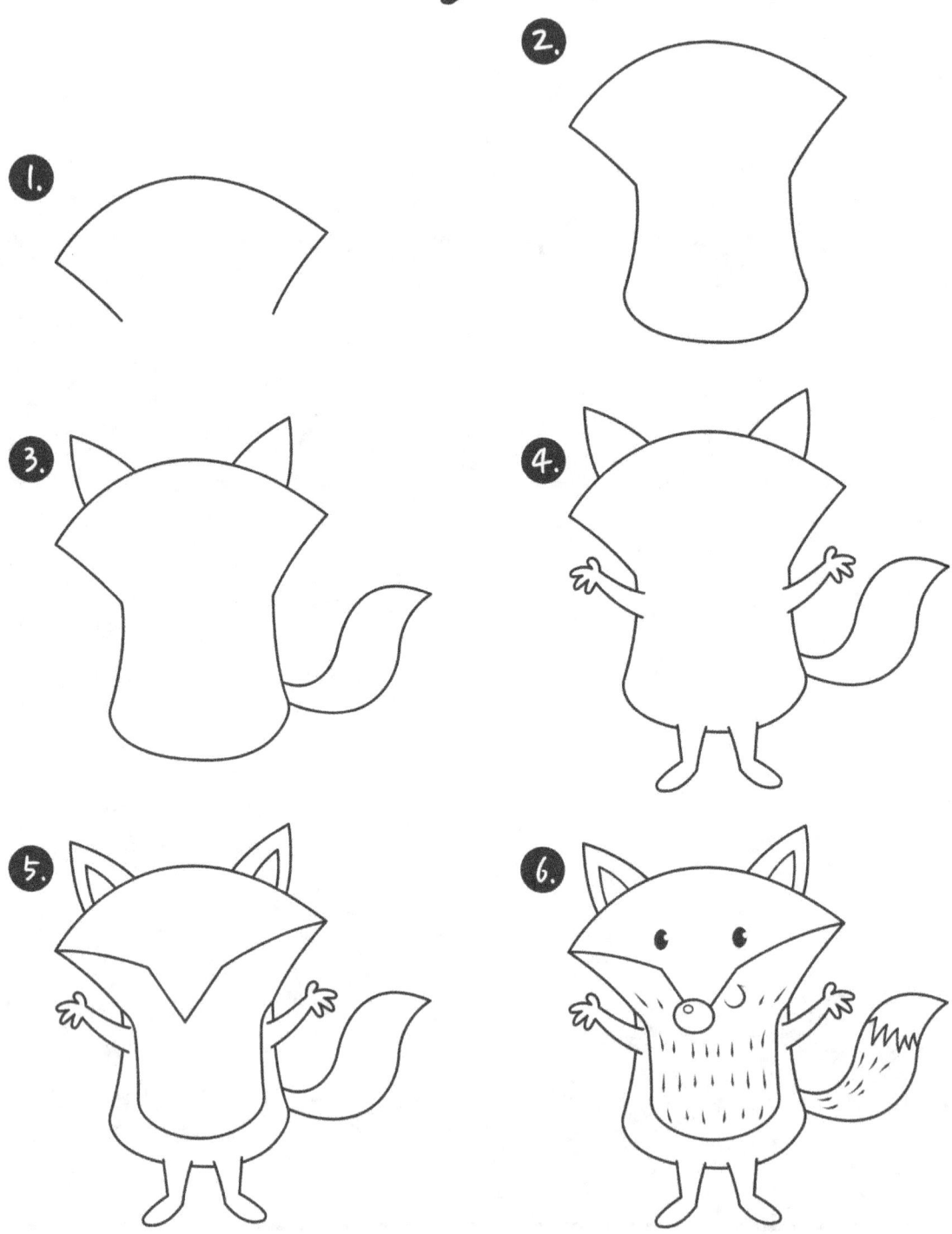

YOUR TURN

How to draw bear butt

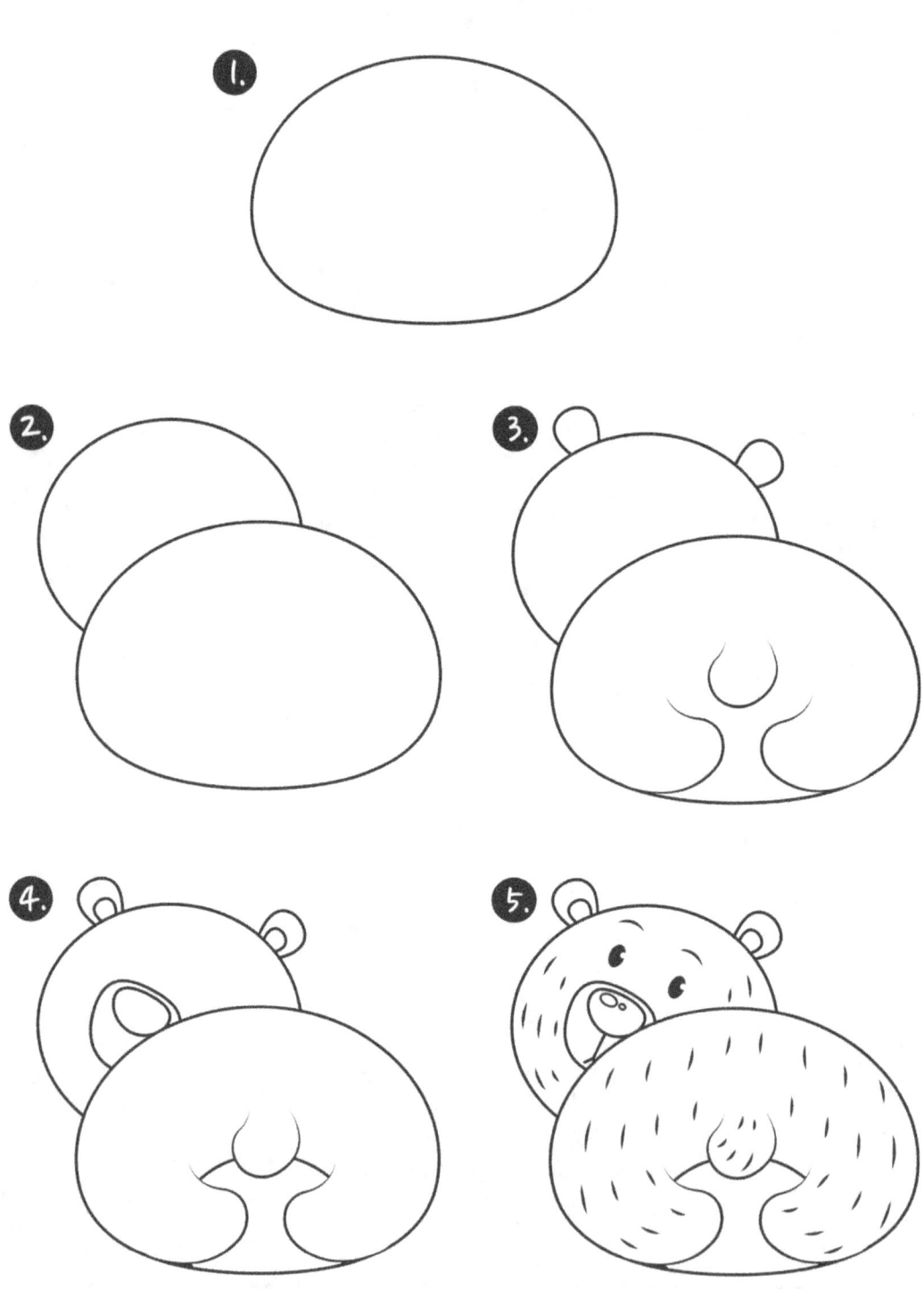

YOUR TURN

How to draw running tiger

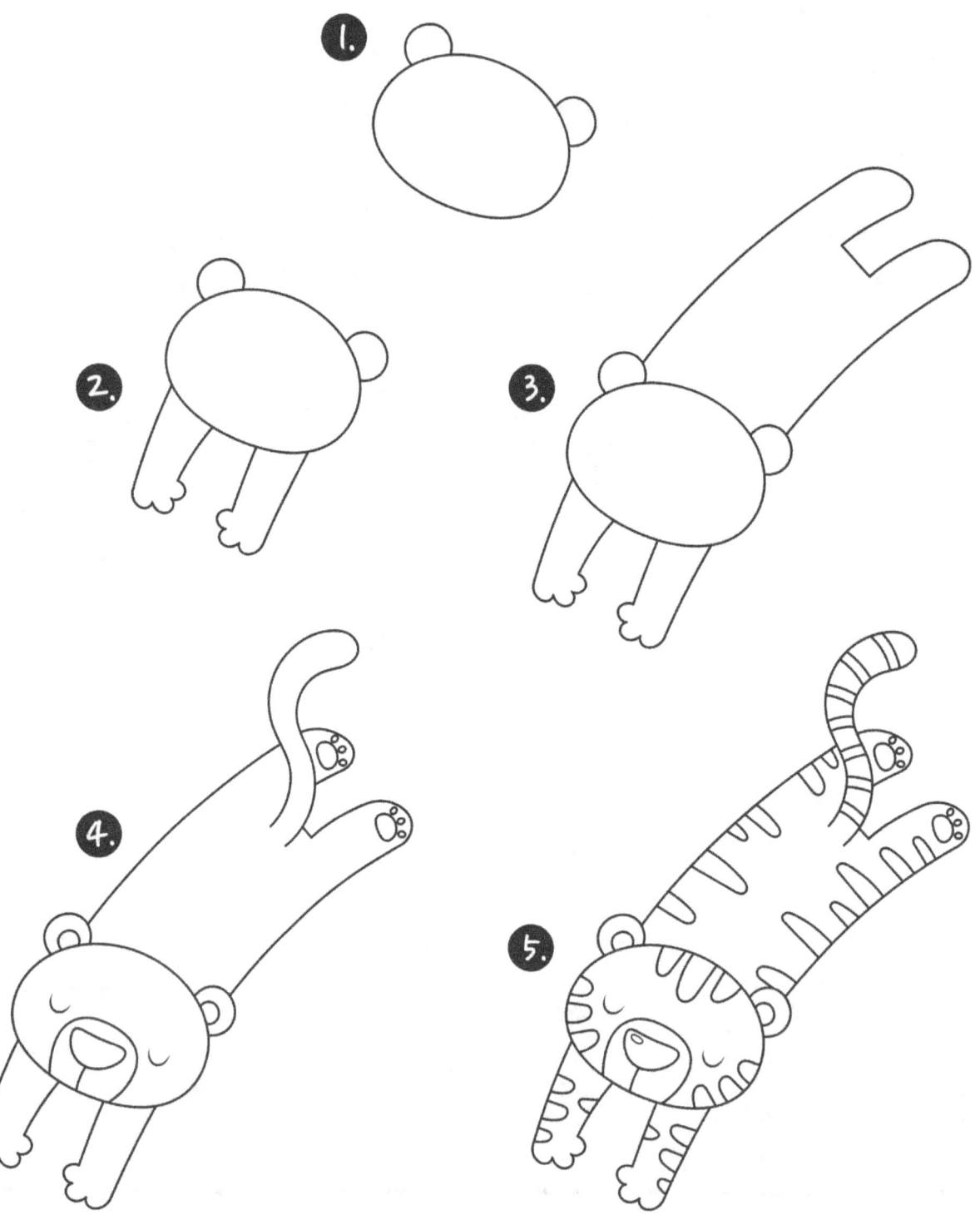

YOUR TURN

How to draw edgy chicken

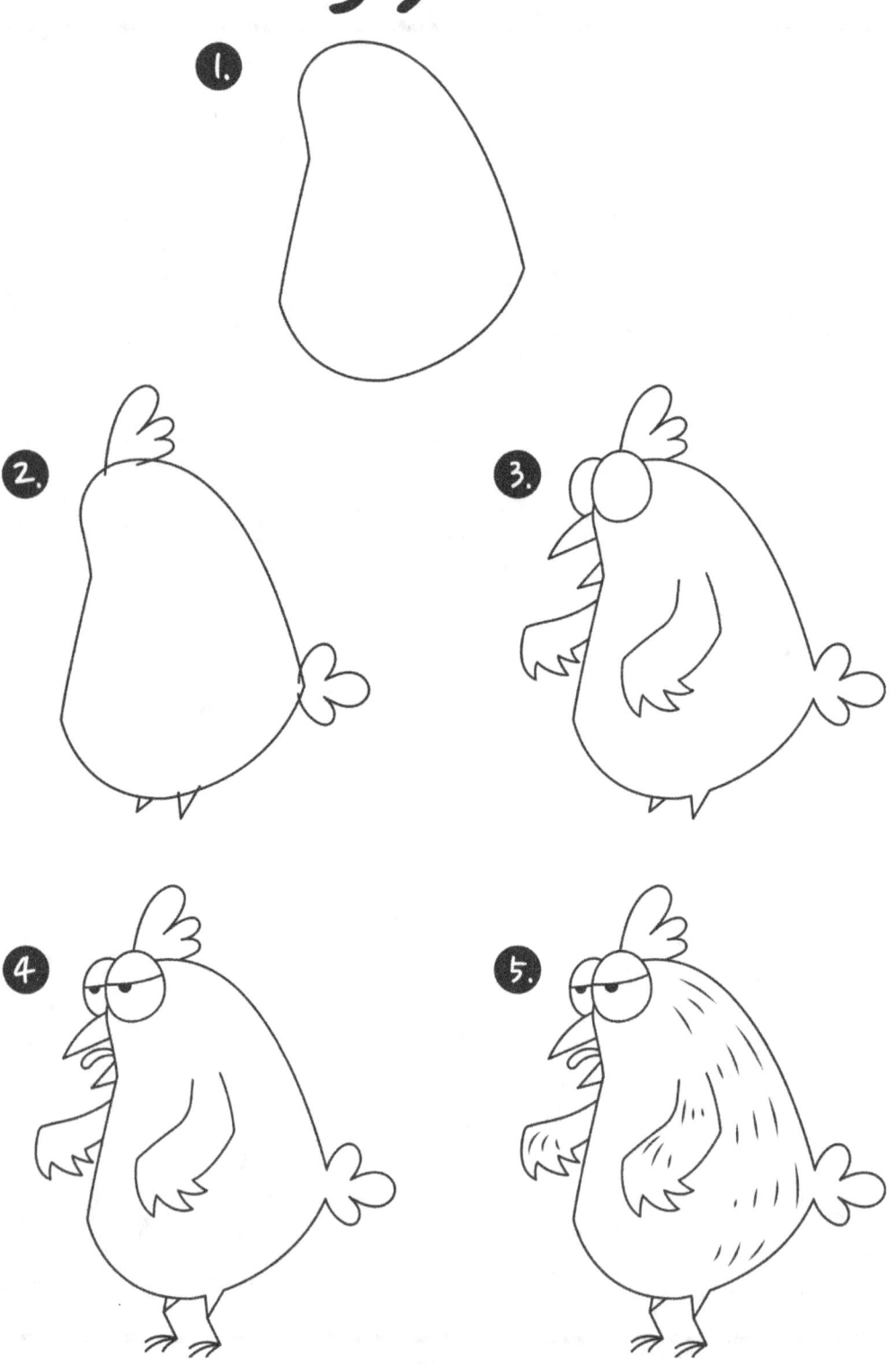

YOUR TURN

How to draw a squirrel

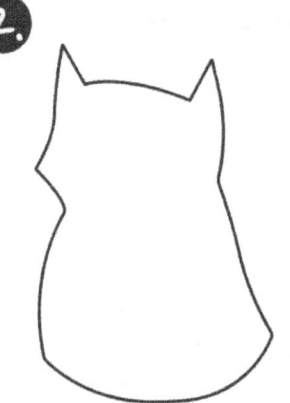
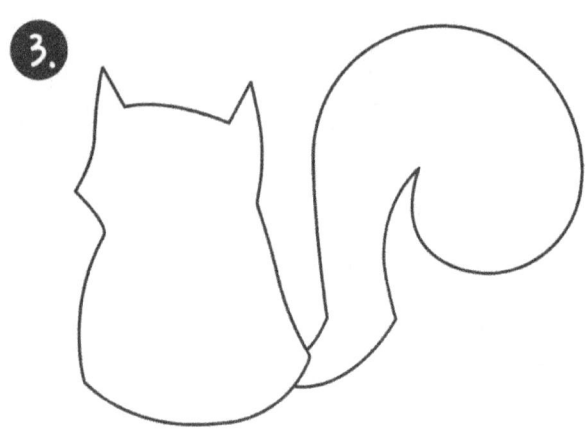
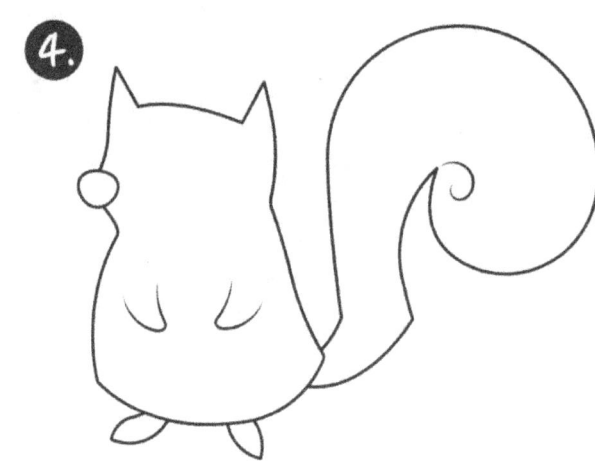
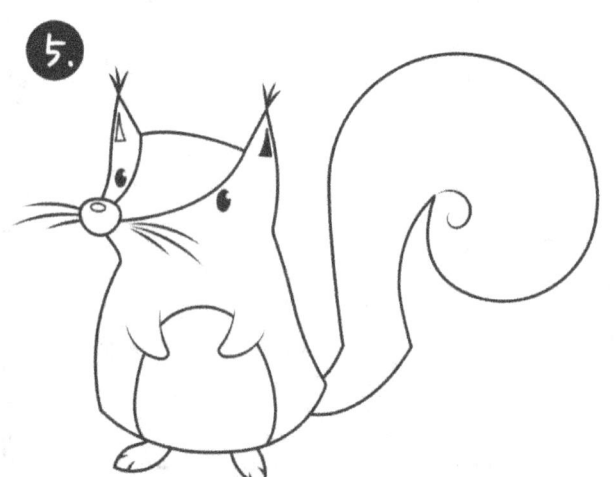
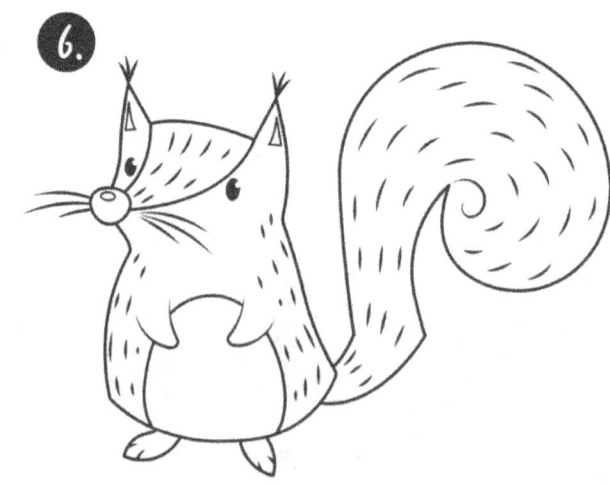

YOUR TURN

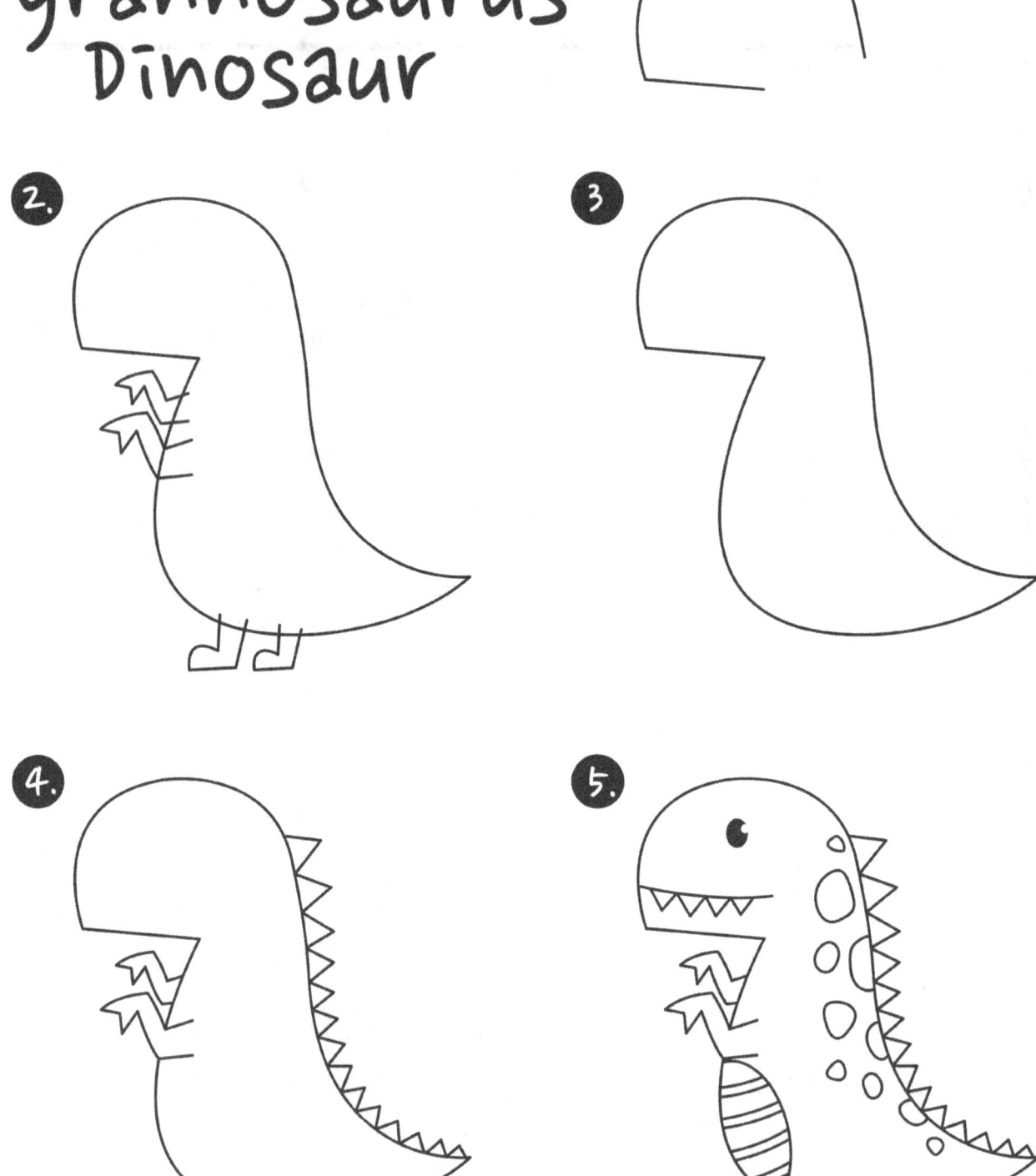

YOUR TURN

How to draw Pteranodon Dinosaur

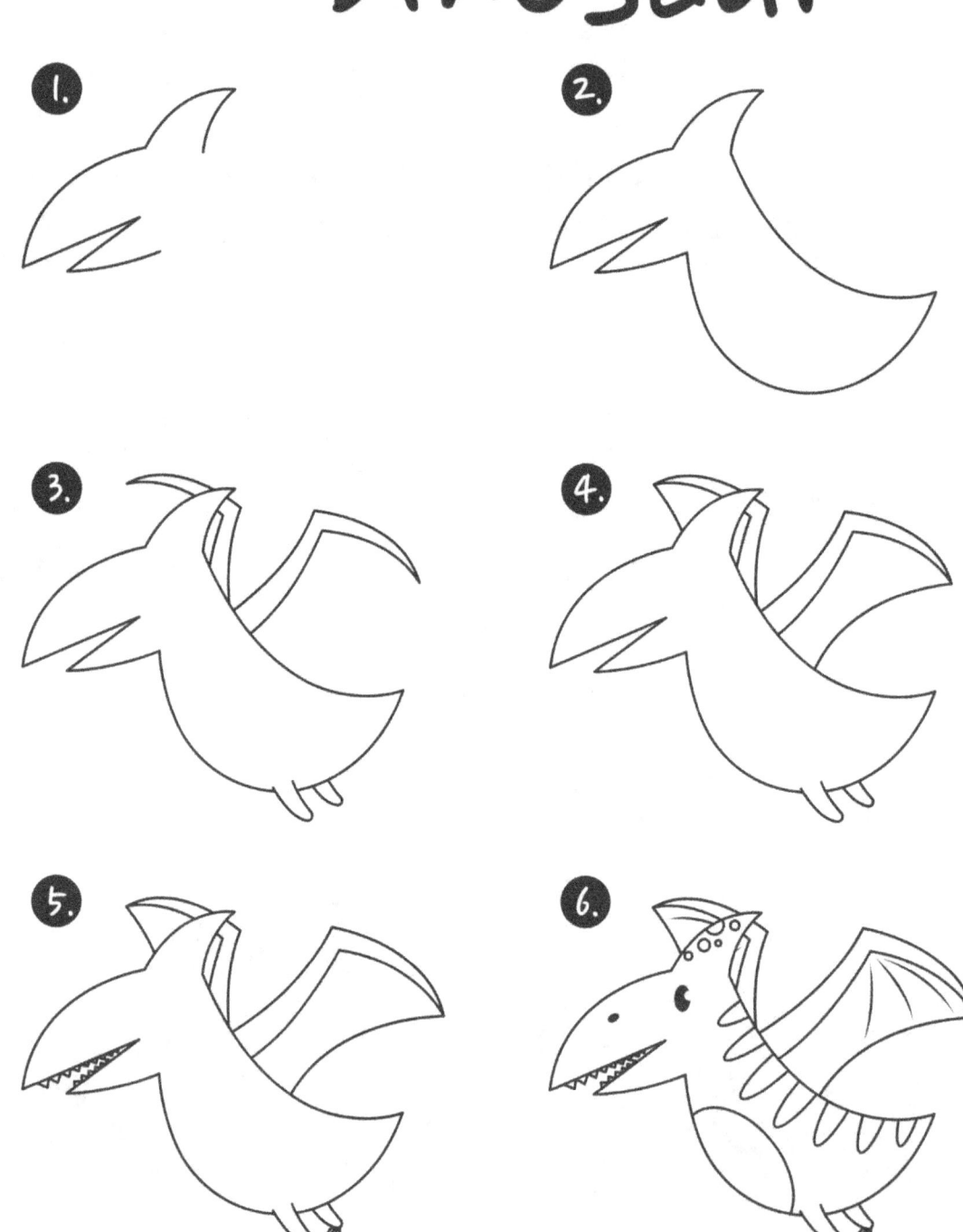

YOUR TURN

How to draw a sleeping lion

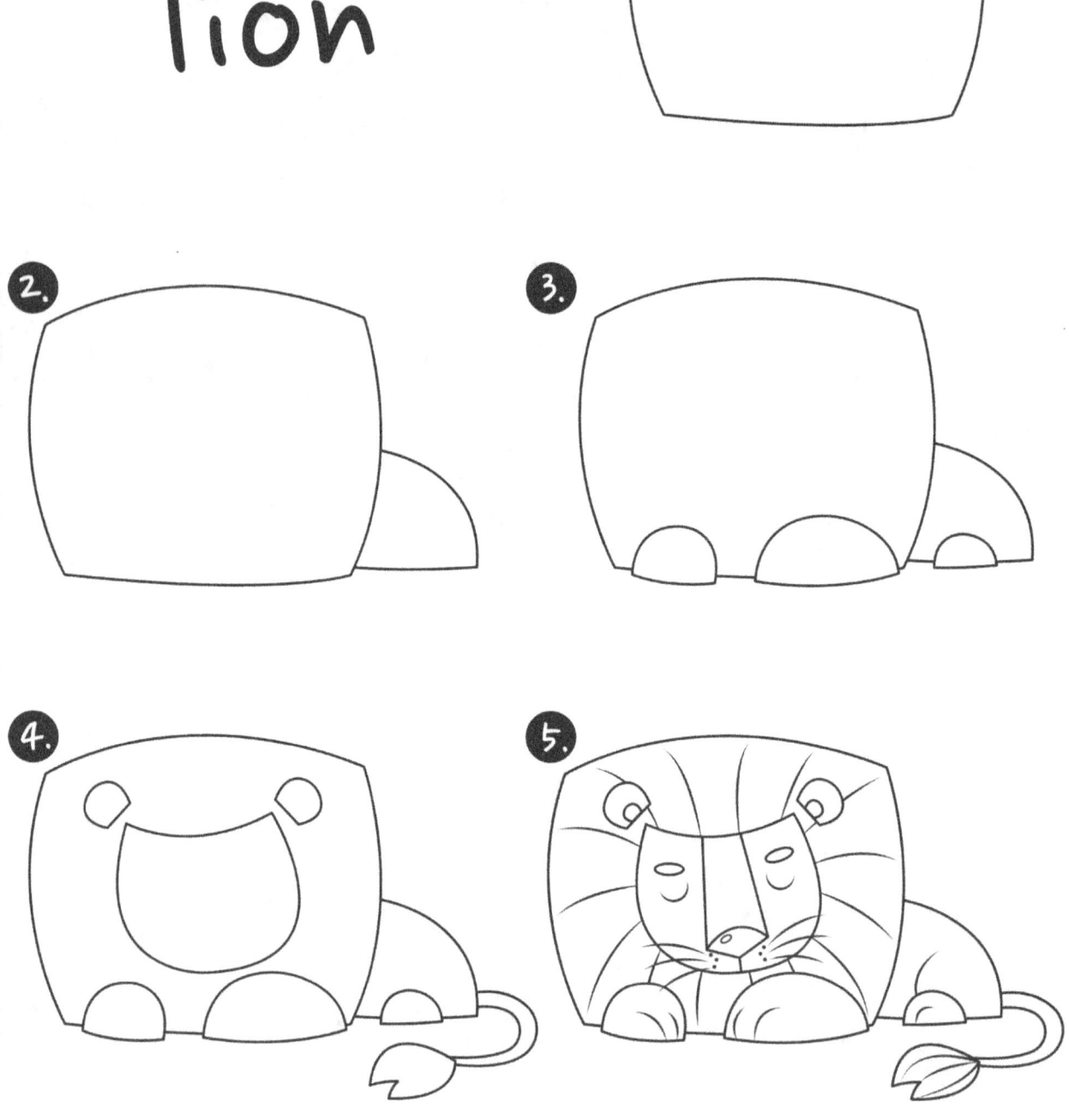

YOUR TURN

How to draw a cockroach

1.

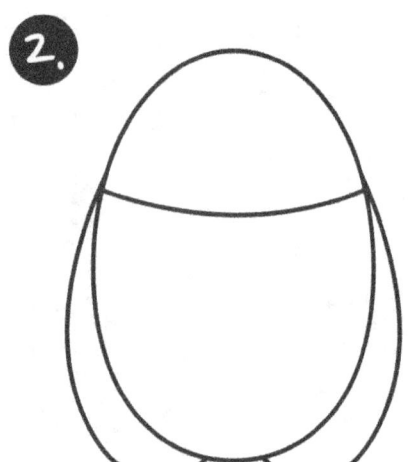
2.

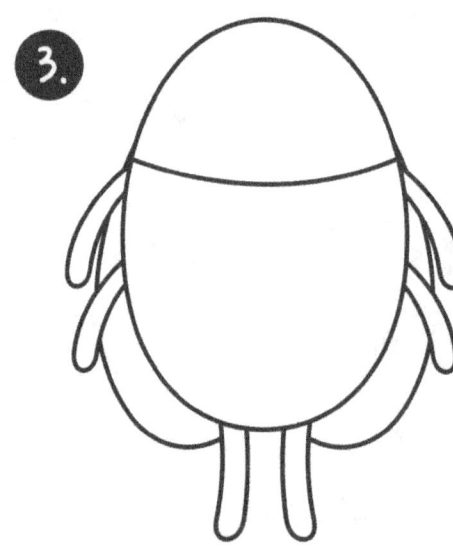
3.

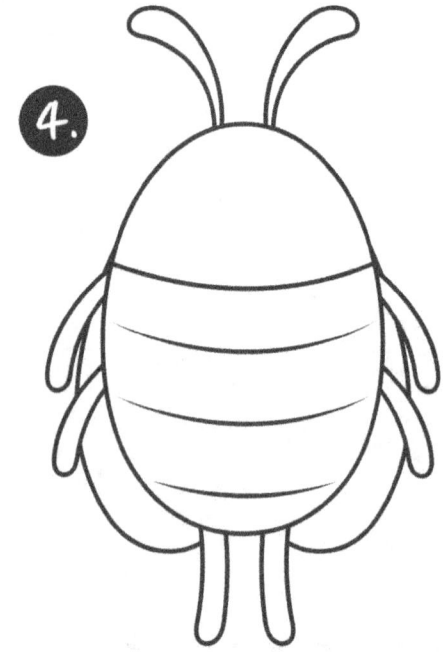
4.

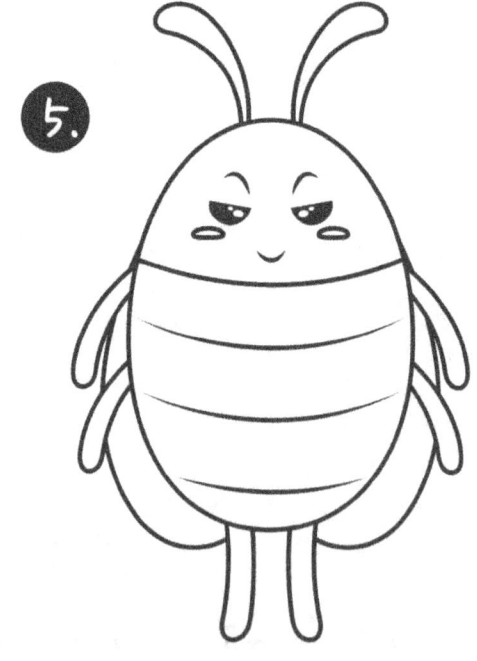
5.

YOUR TURN

How to draw a puffer fish

1.

2.

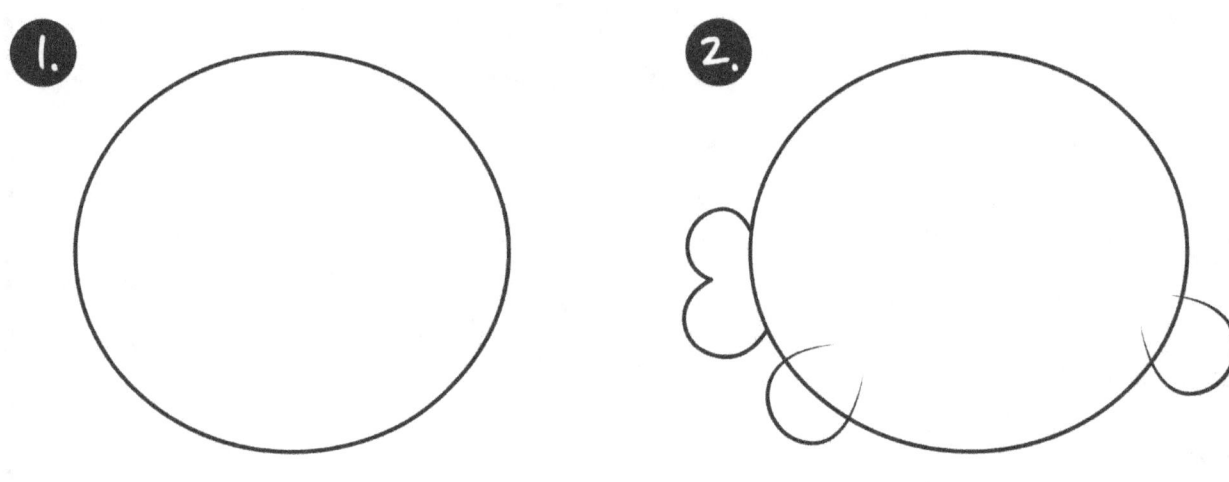

3.

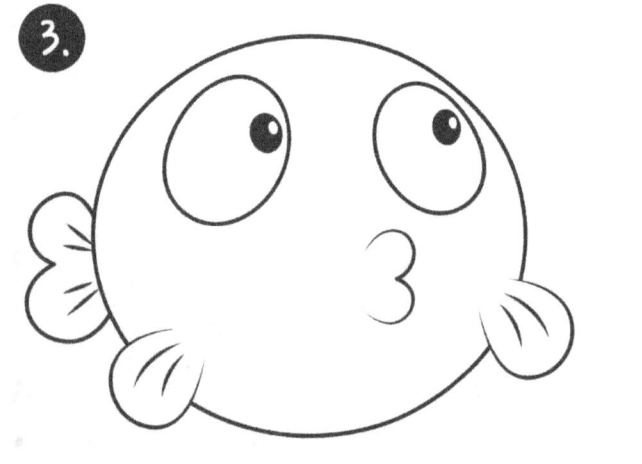

4.

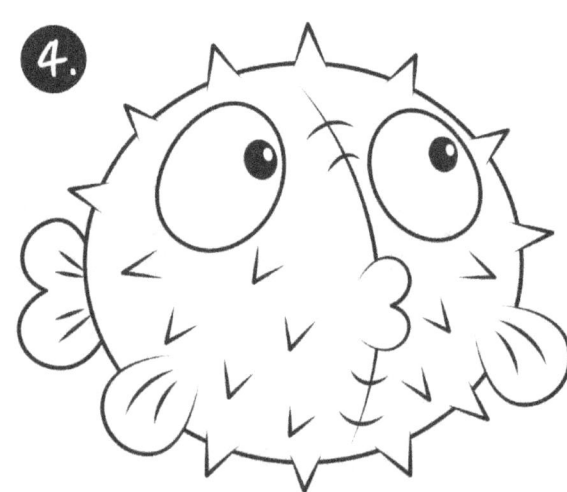

YOUR TURN

How to draw an elephant

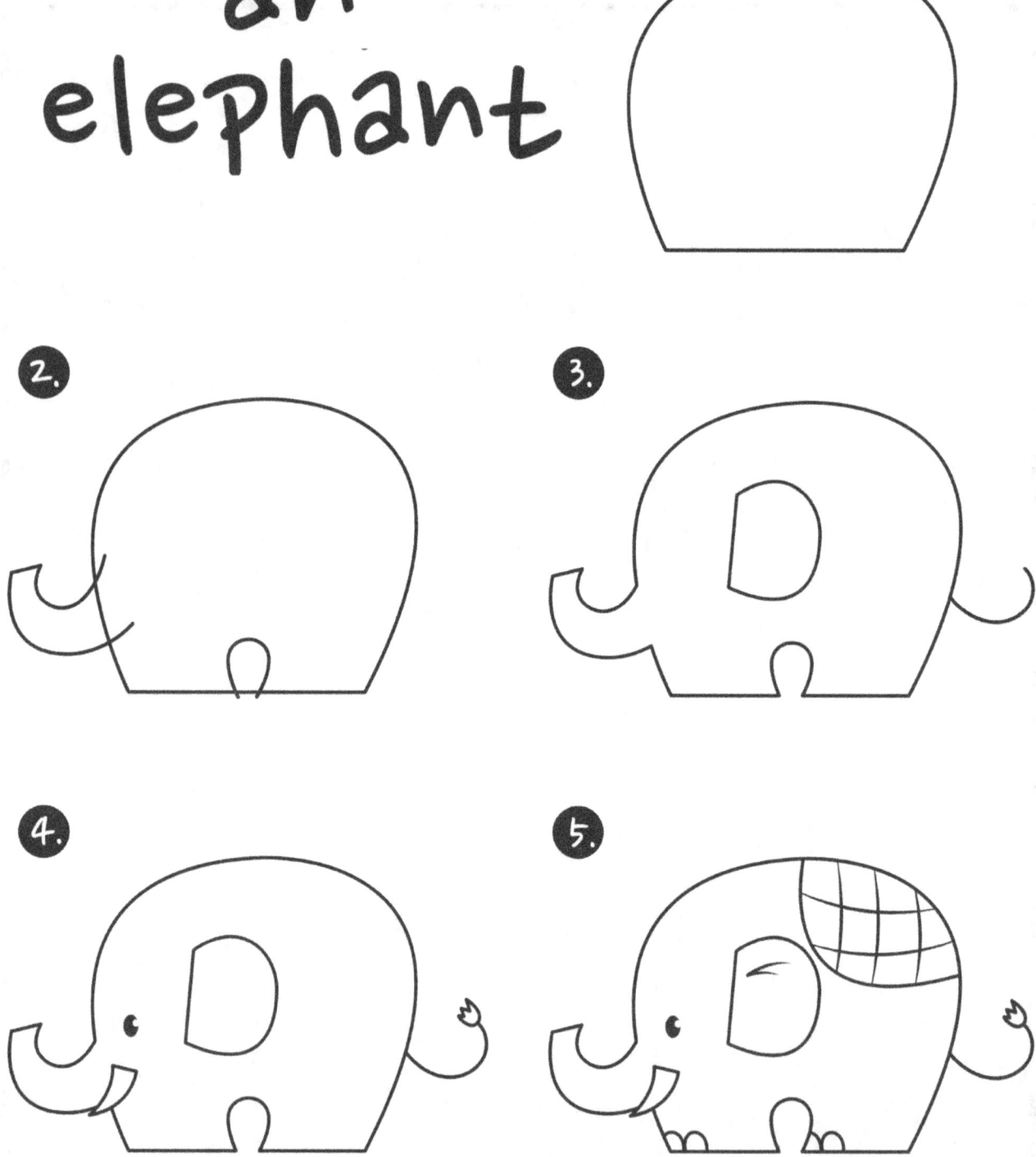

YOUR TURN

How to draw a sheep

1.
2.
3.
4.
5.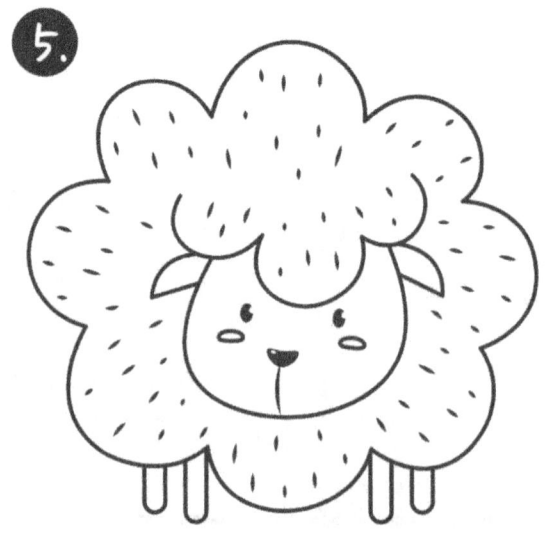

YOUR TURN

How to draw a monkey

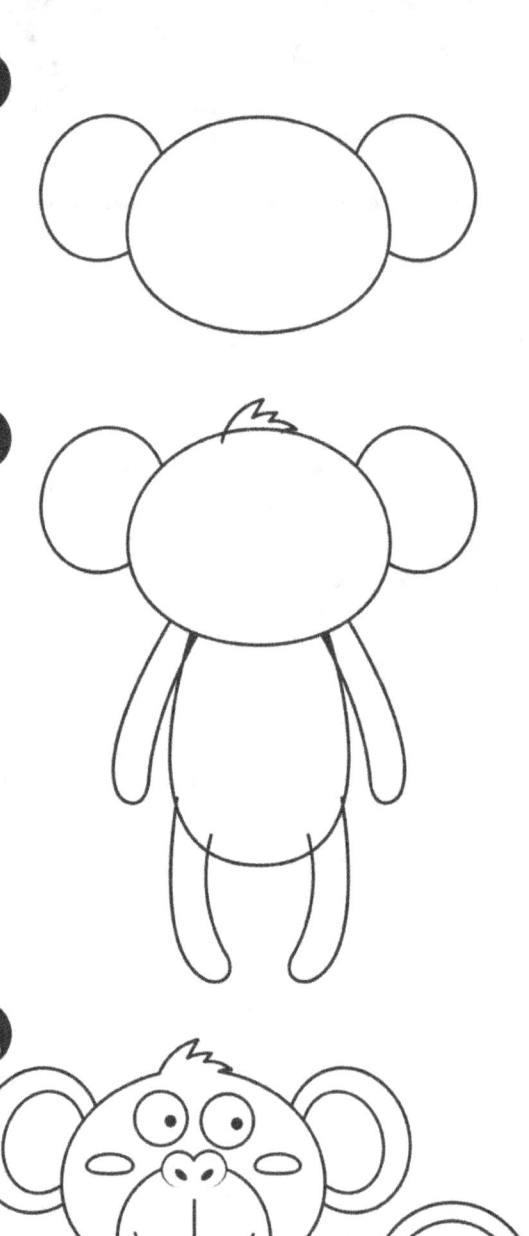
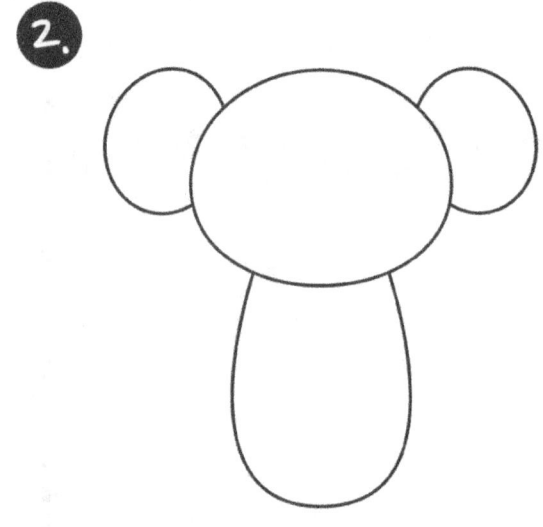
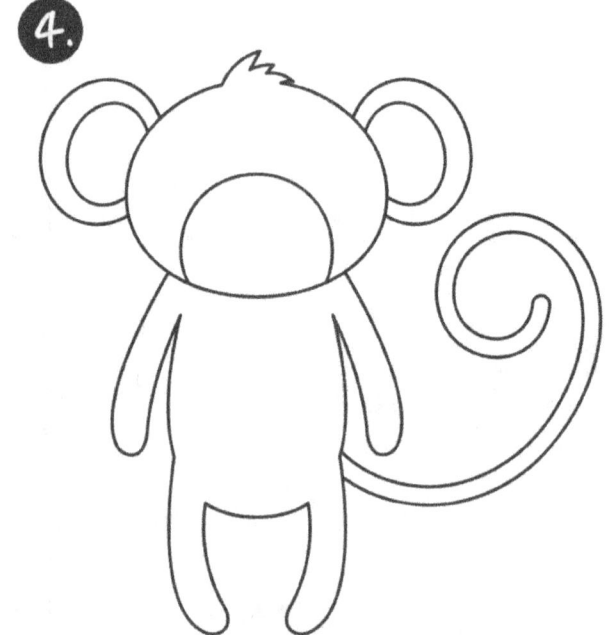
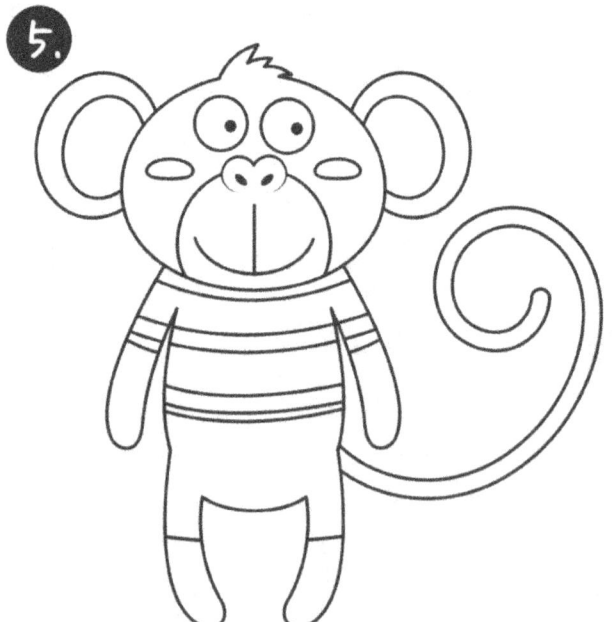

YOUR TURN

How to draw a porcupine

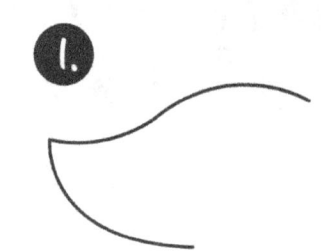

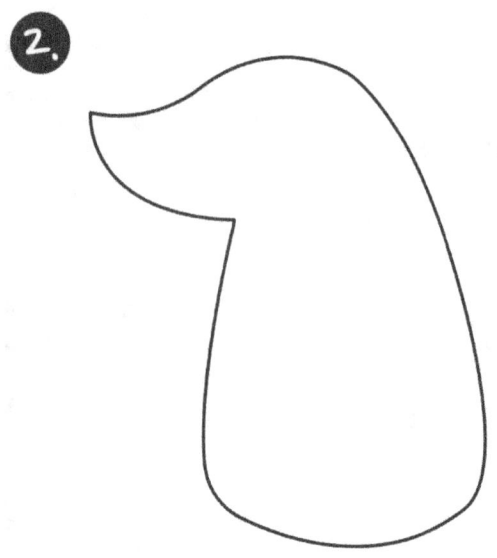

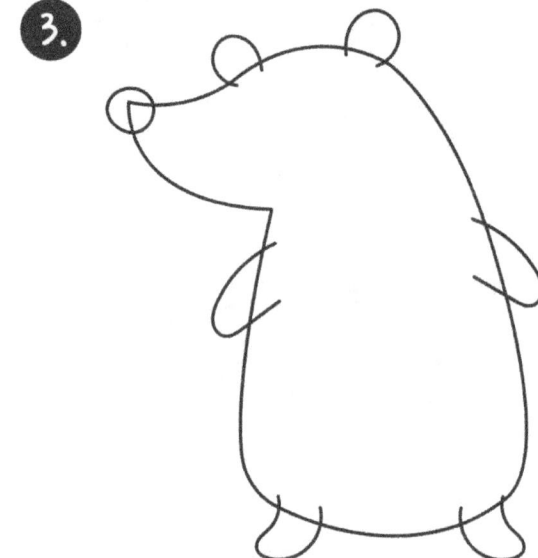

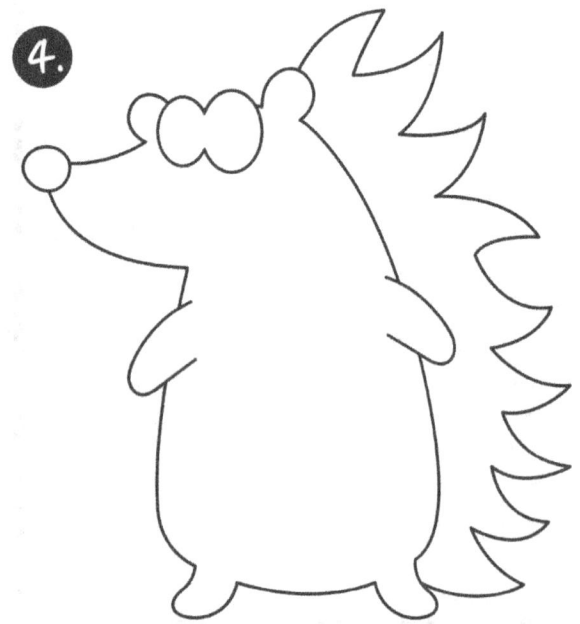

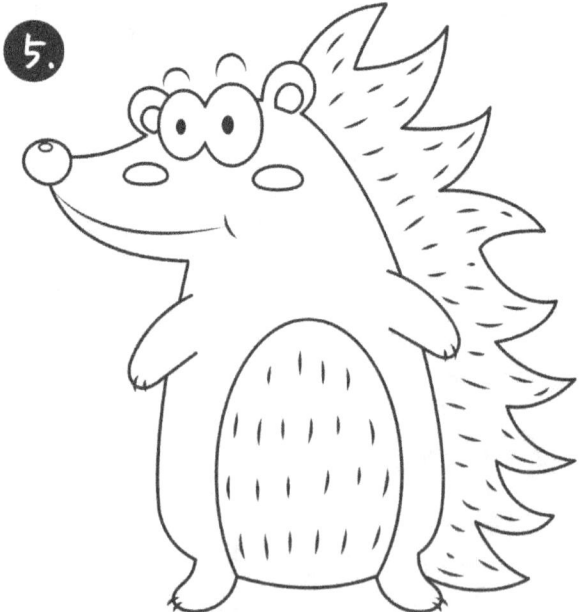

YOUR TURN

How to draw a buffalo

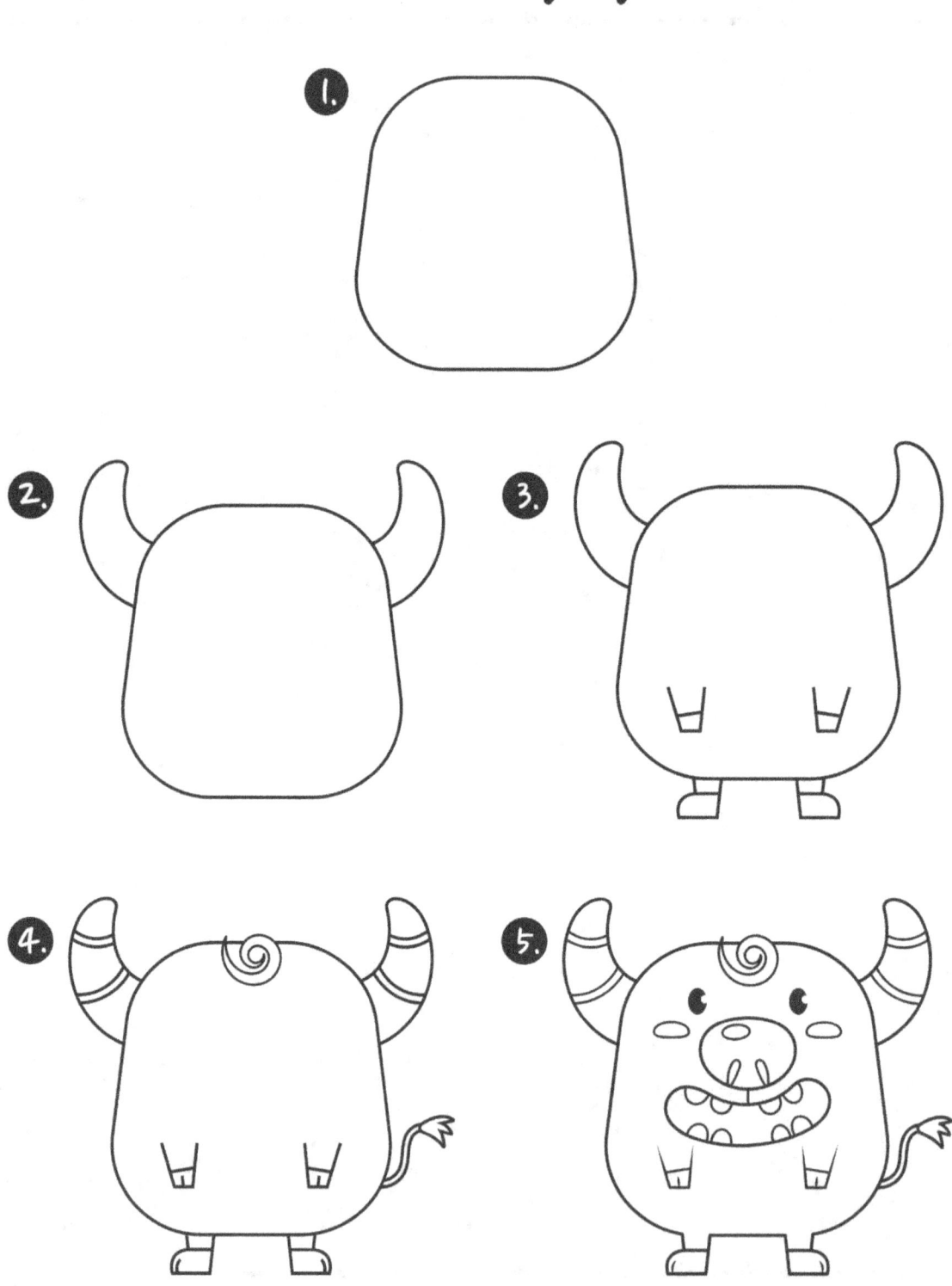

YOUR TURN

How to draw a doggy

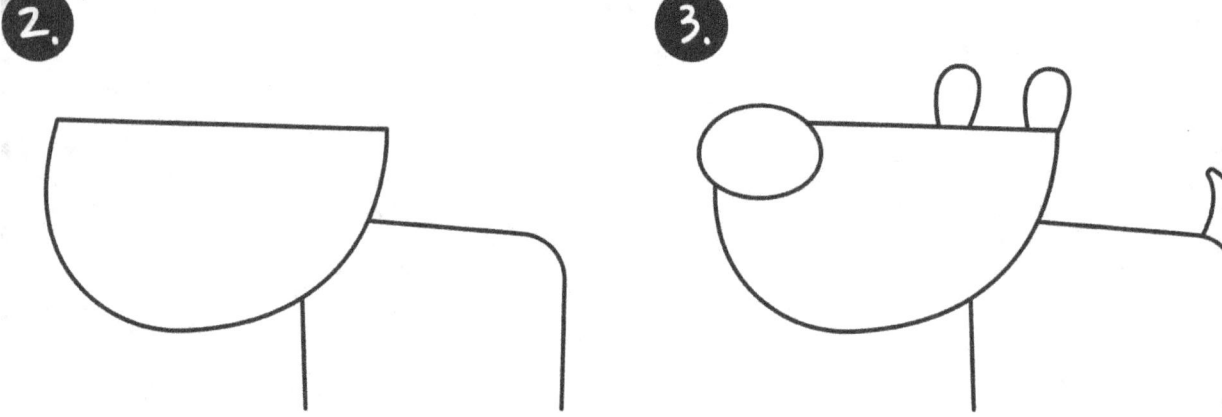
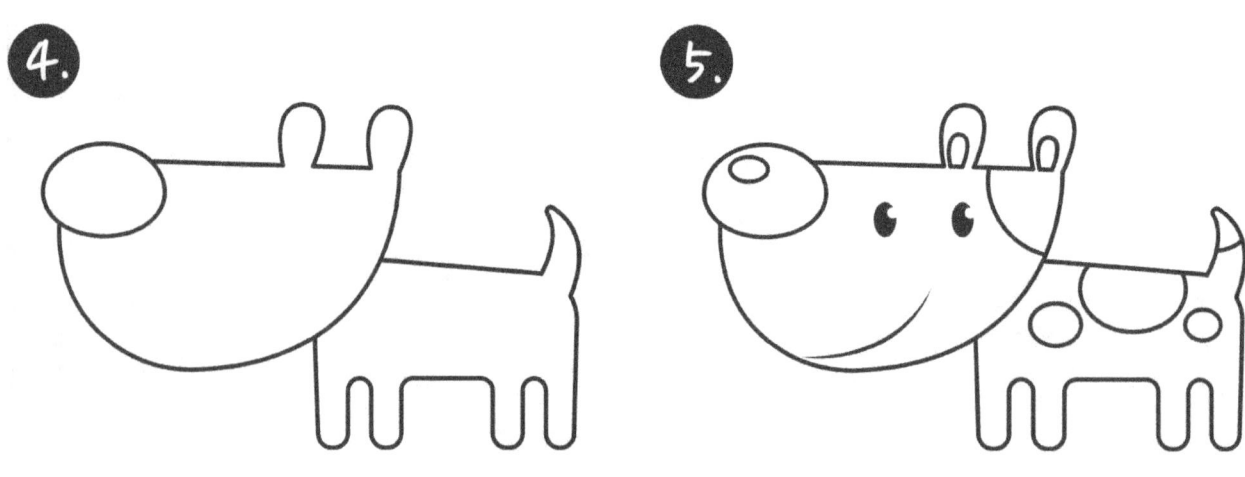

YOUR TURN

How to draw a whale

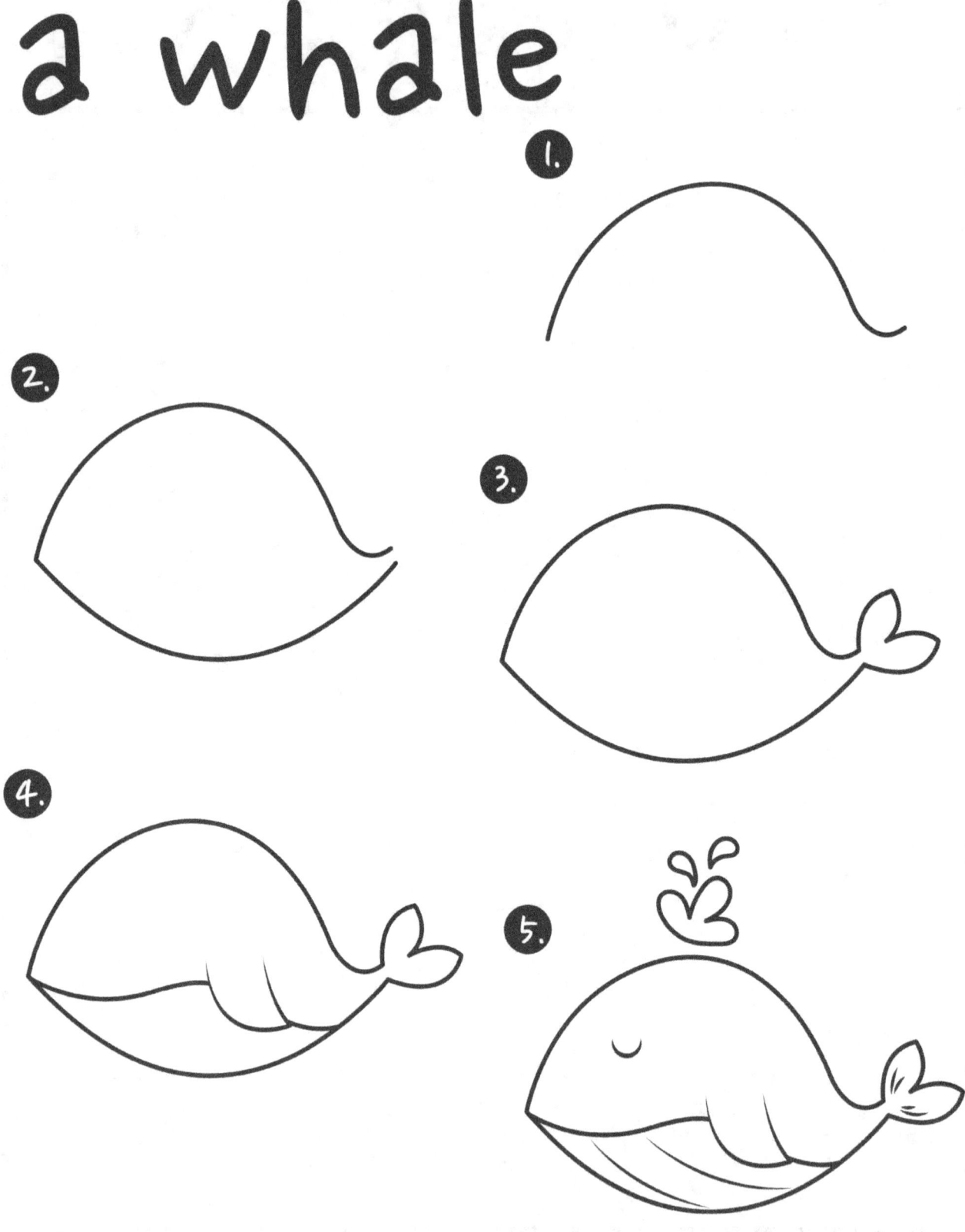

YOUR TURN

How to draw a little bird

1.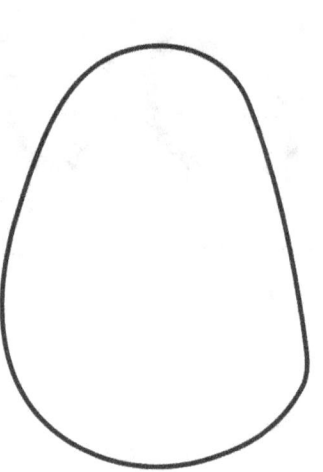
2.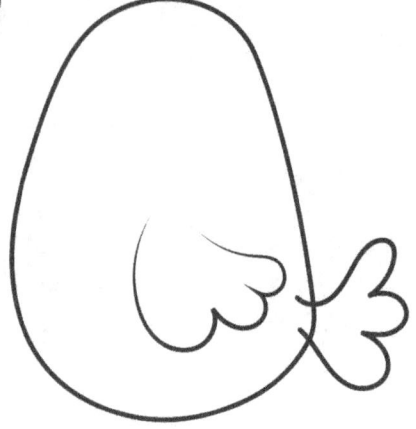
3.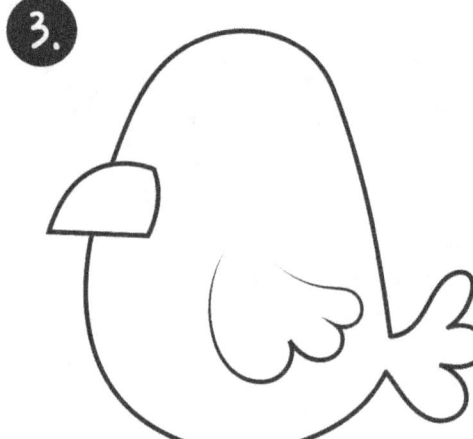
4.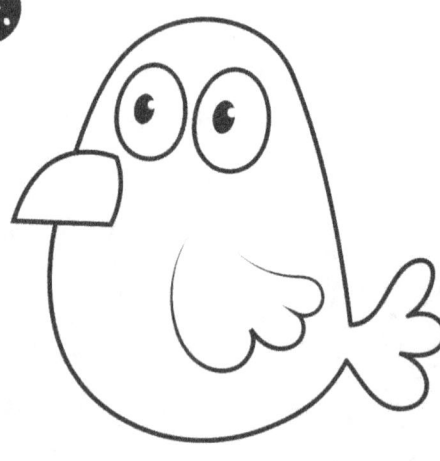
5.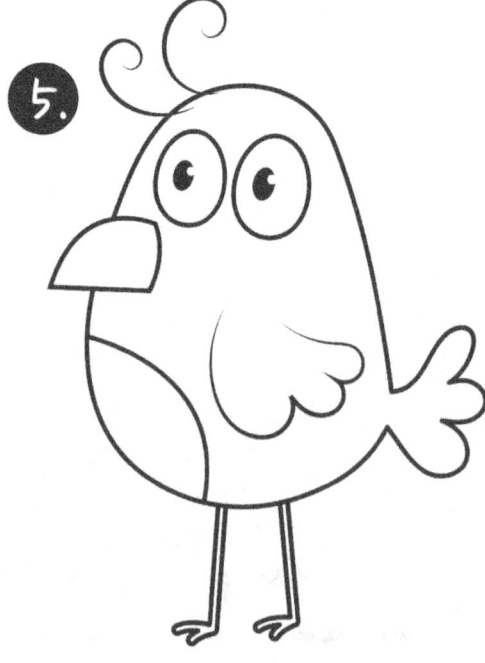

YOUR TURN

How to draw a PUPPY

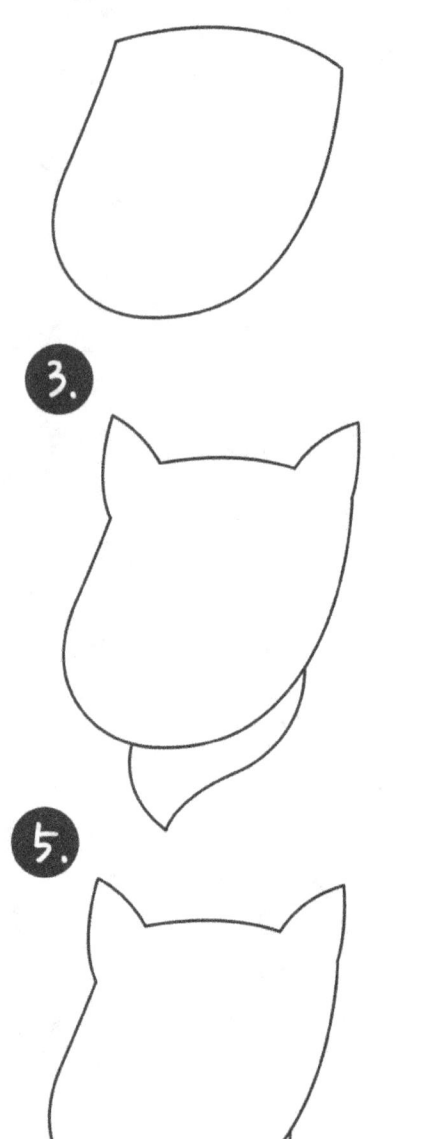
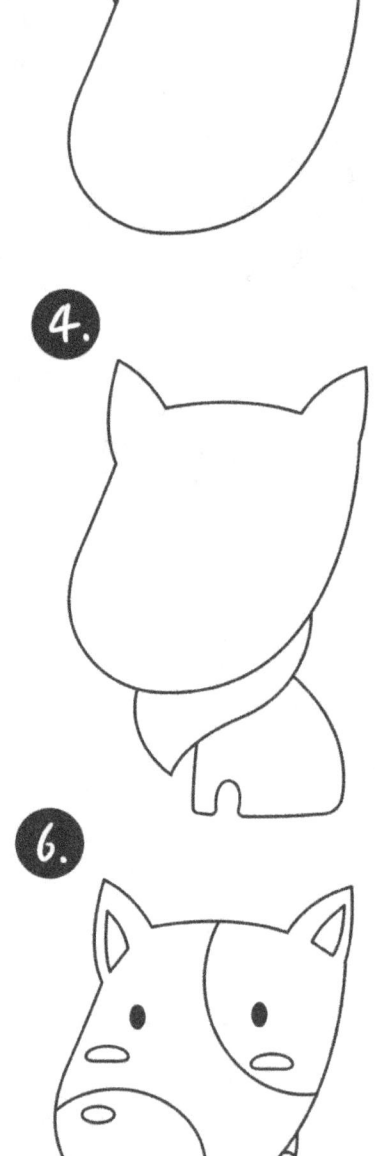
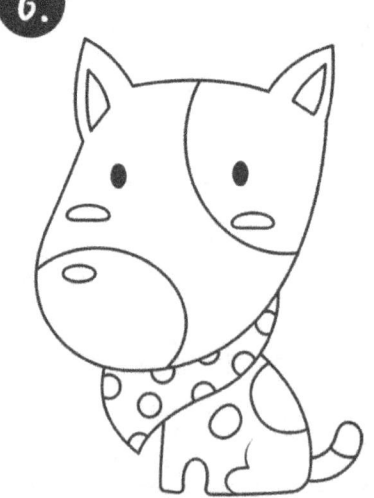

YOUR TURN

How to draw a squirrel

1.
2.
3.
4.
5.
6.

YOUR TURN

How to draw a fox

1.
2.
3.
4.
5.

YOUR TURN

How to draw a lion

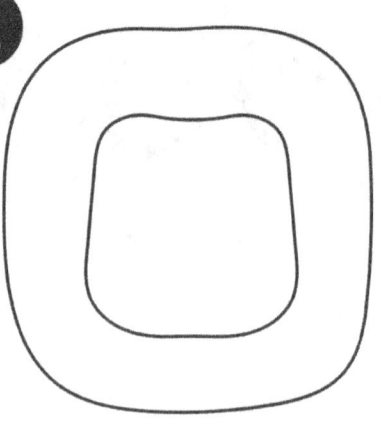
1.

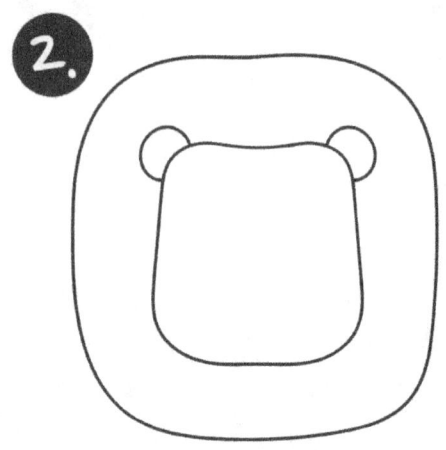
2.

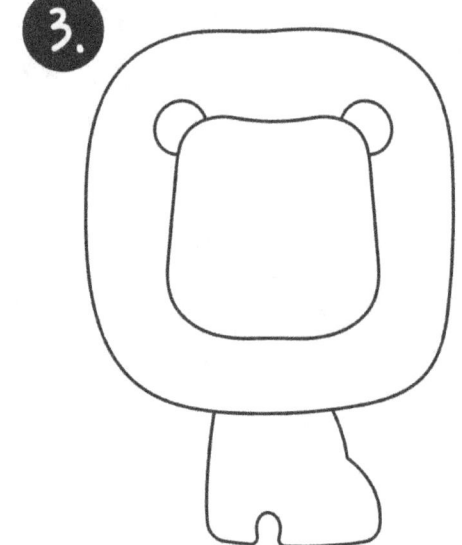
3.

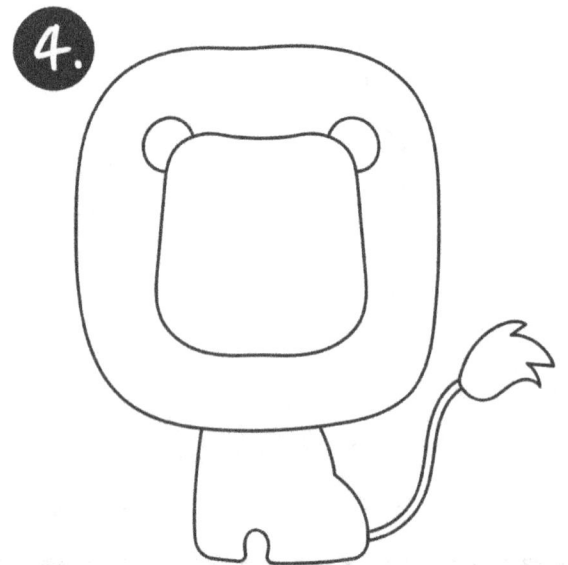
4.

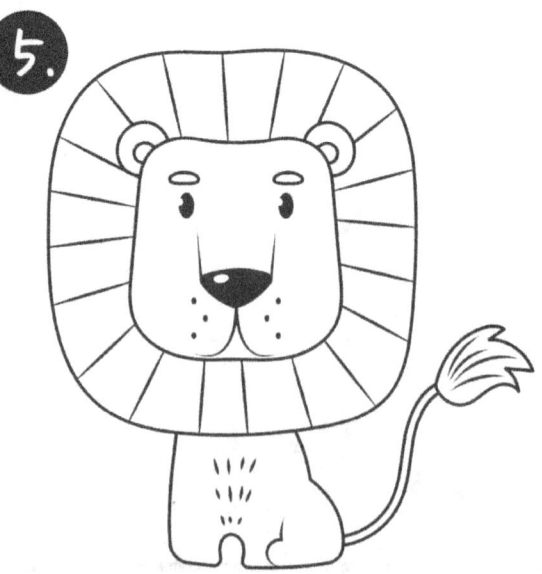
5.

YOUR TURN

How to draw a cat

1.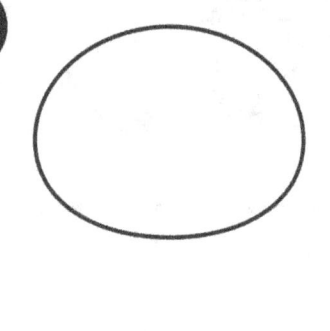

2.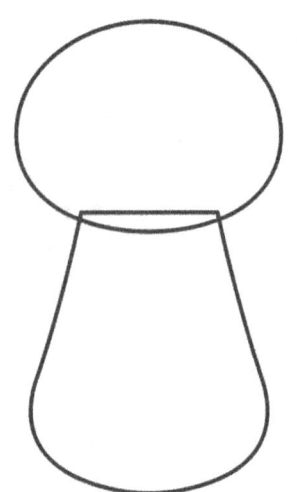

3.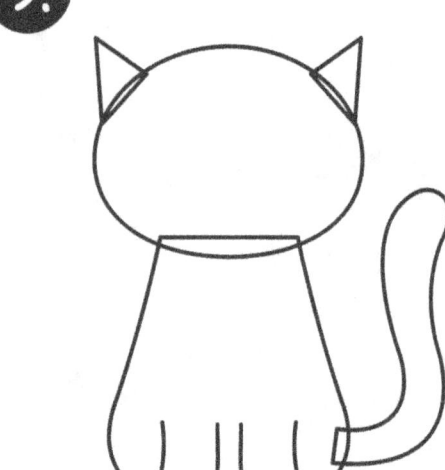

4.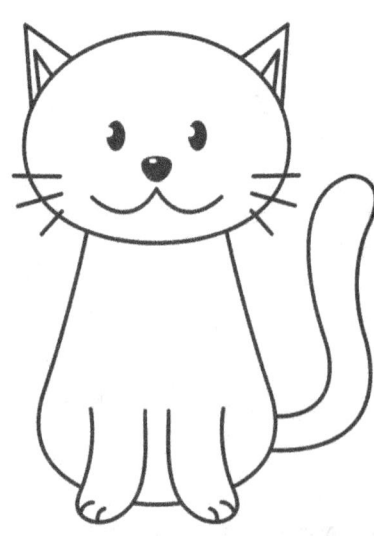

5.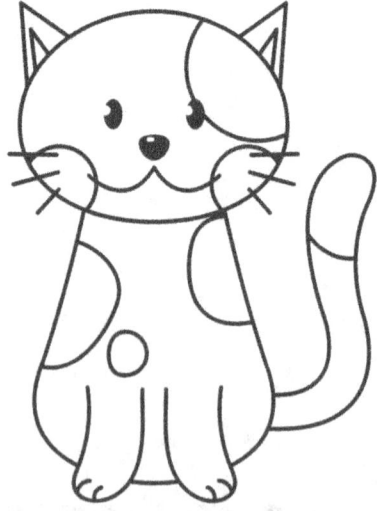

YOUR TURN

How to draw a bear

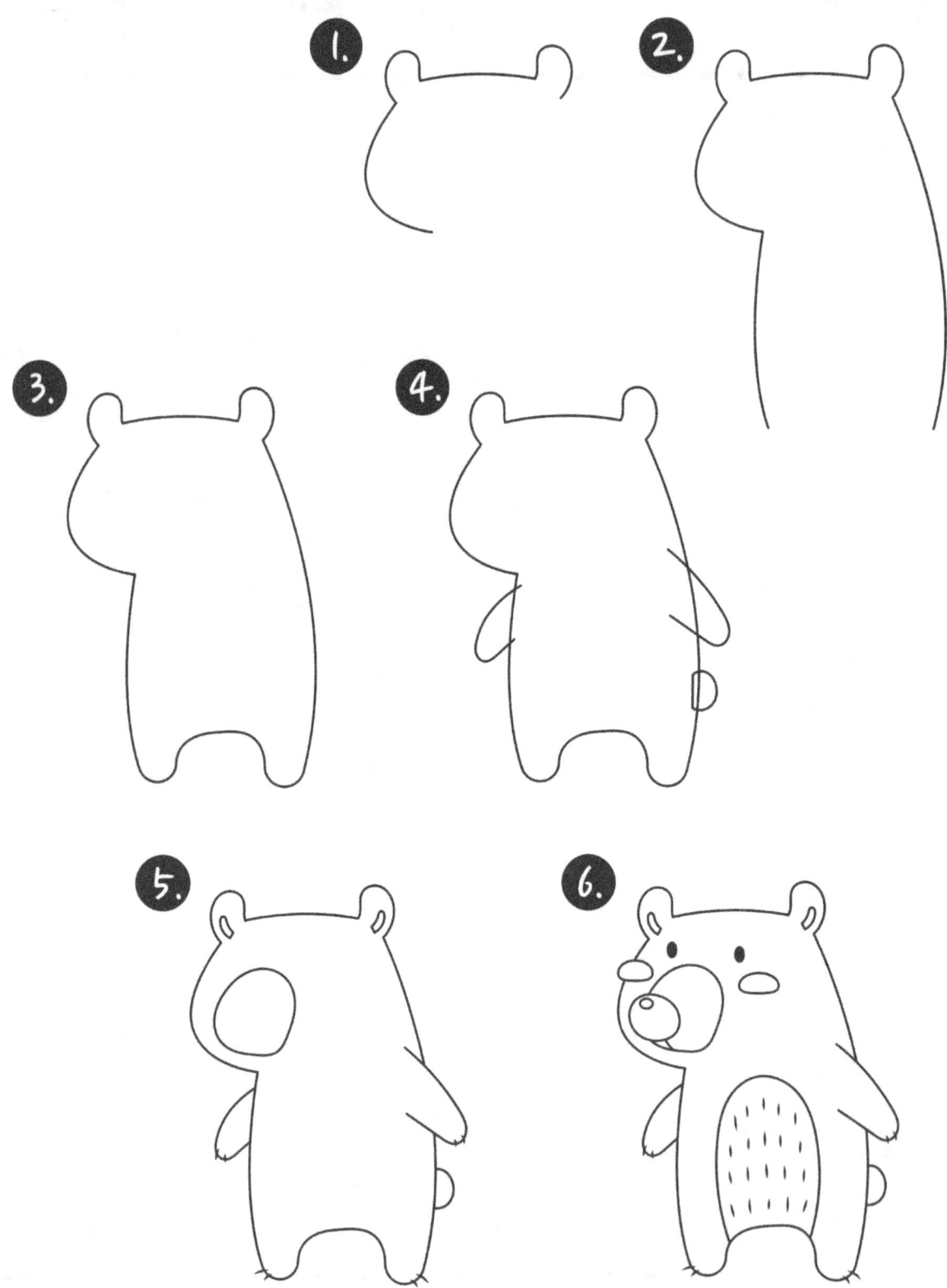

YOUR TURN

How to draw a funny bee

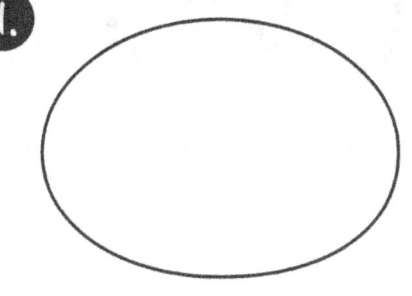
1.

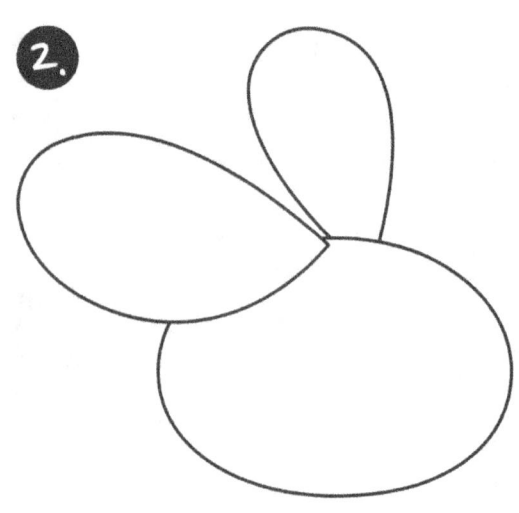
2.

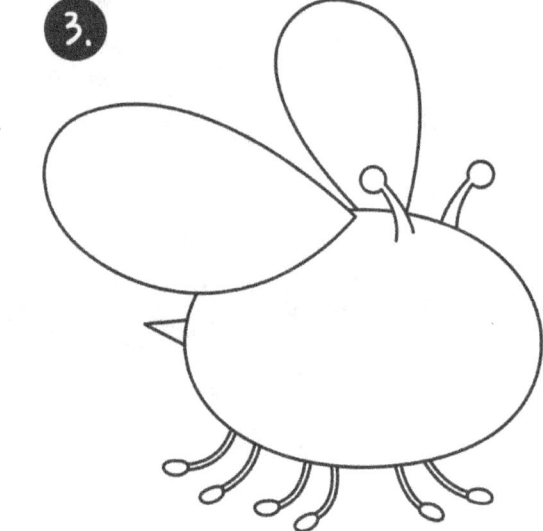
3.

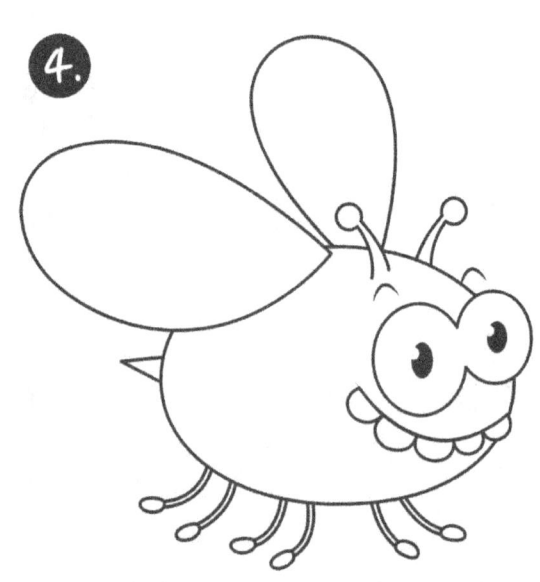
4.

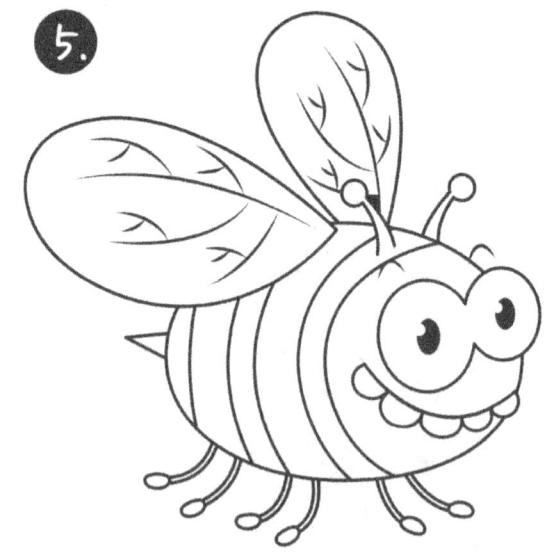
5.

YOUR TURN

How to draw a crab

1.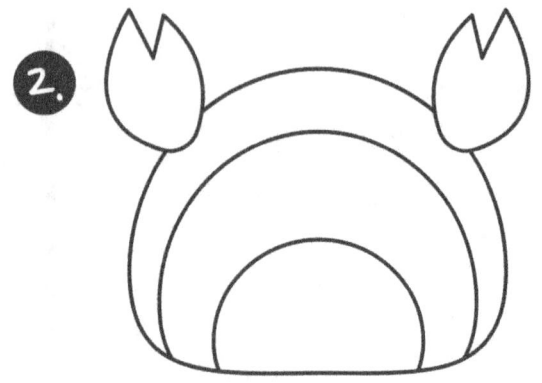

2.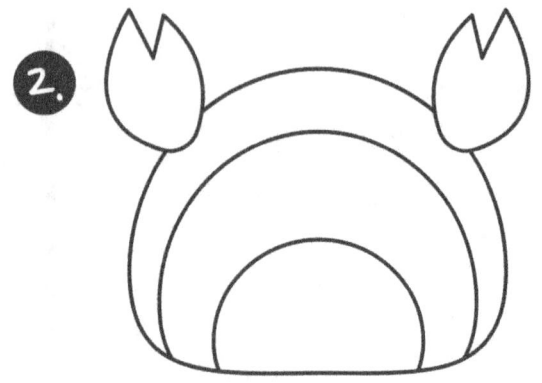

3.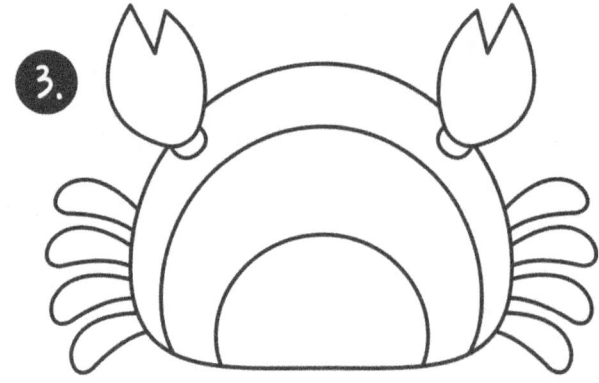

4.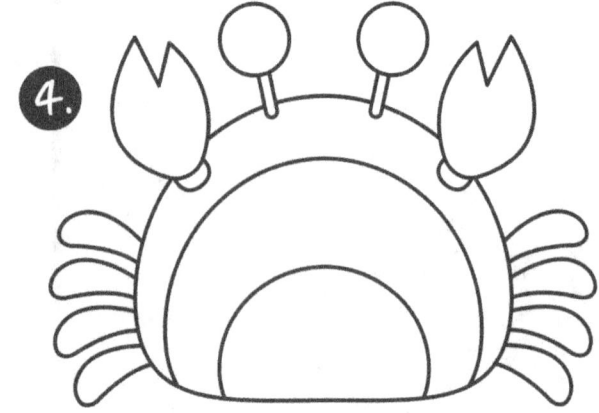

5.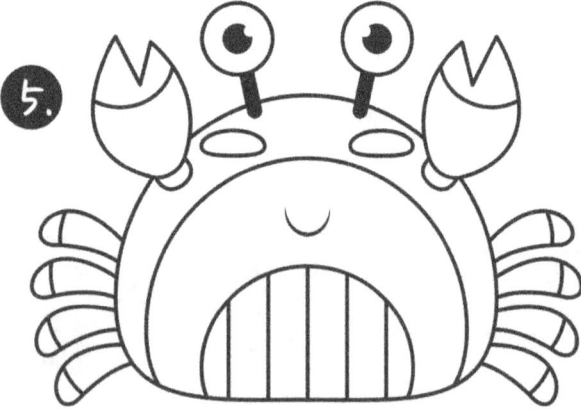

YOUR TURN

How to draw sea otter

1.
2.
3.
4.
5.

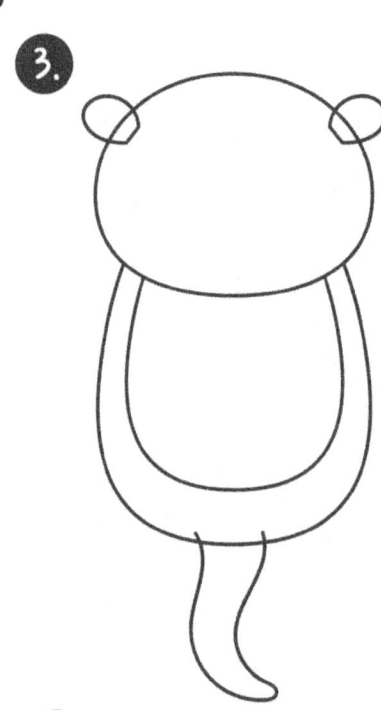
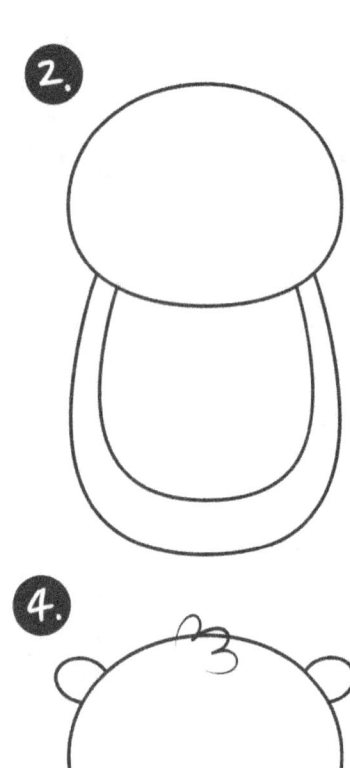
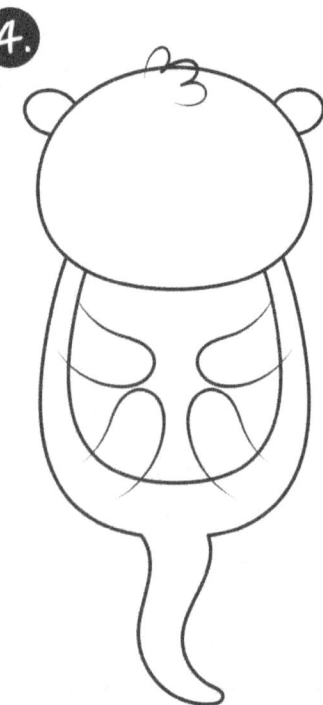
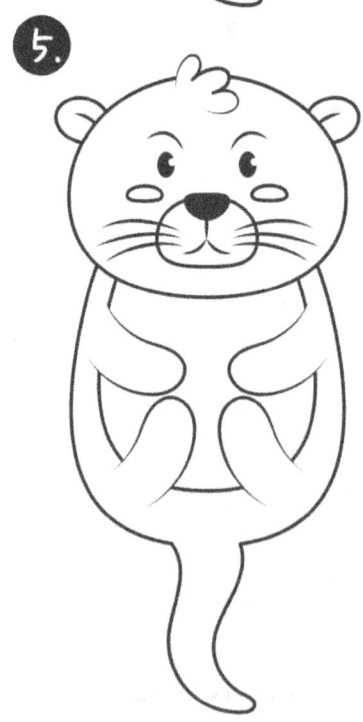

YOUR TURN

How to draw iguana

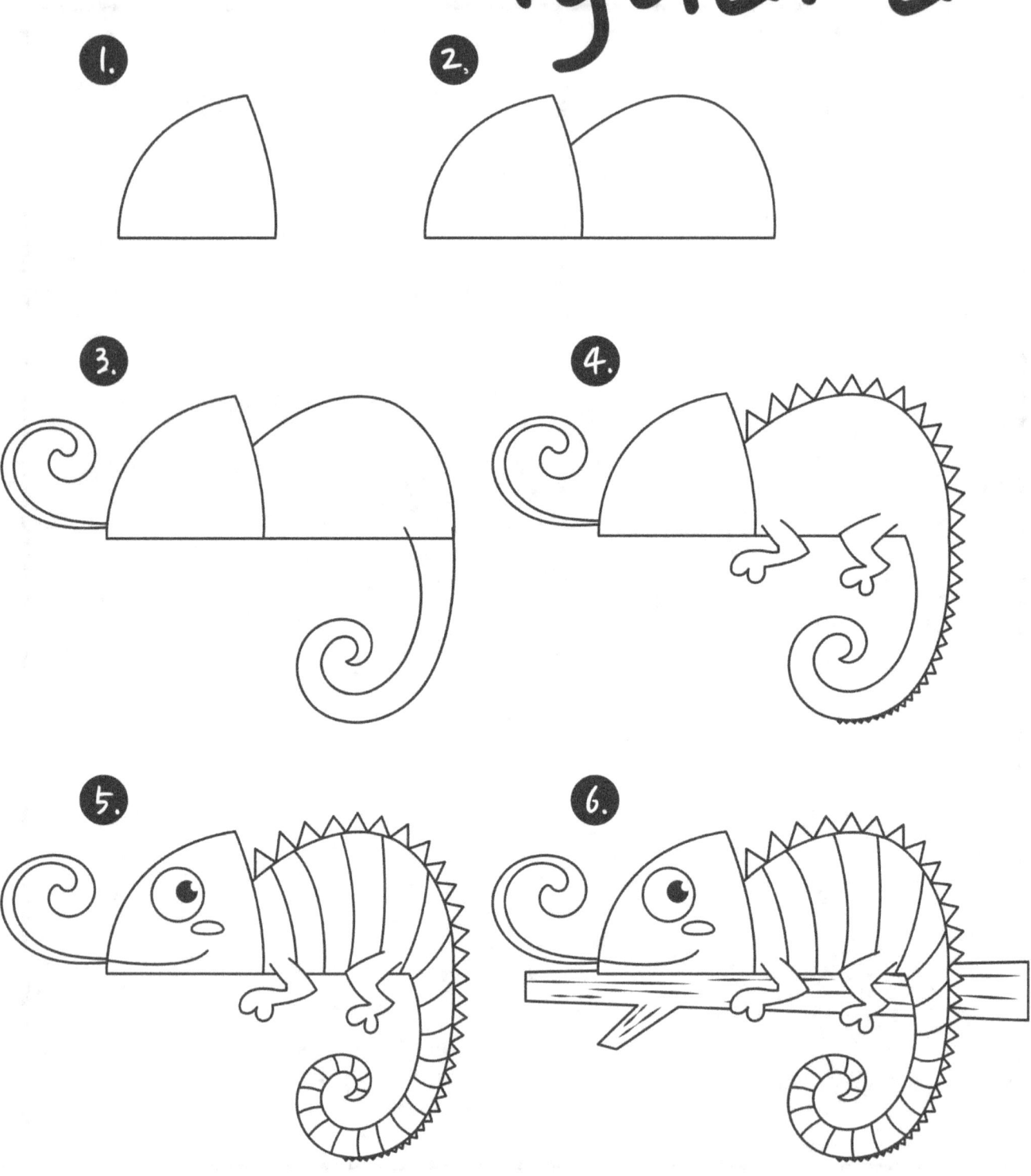

YOUR TURN

Thank You